74 Short Plays for Starting
Discussions with Teenagers

ACTING
IT OUT

Joan Sturkie & Marsh Cassady

Resource Publications, Inc. • San Jose, California

Editorial director: Kenneth Guentert
Production editor: Kathi Drolet
Art director: Terri Ysseldyke-All
Editorial assistants: Elizabeth J. Asborno and Gail Mihara

Reprint Department,
Resource Publications, Inc.
160 E. Virginia Street #290
San Jose, CA 95112-5876

Library of Congress Cataloging in Publication Data

Sturkie, Joan.
   Acting it out: 74 short plays for starting discussions with
teenagers / Joan Sturkie and Marsh Cassady.
   Includes bibliographical references.
   ISBN 0-89390-178-4
   1. Teenagers—Conduct of life—Drama. 2. Young adult drama,
American. 3. One-act plays, American. I. Cassady, Marsh. II. Title.
PS3569.T879A64 1990
812'.54—dc20   90-35353

Printed in the United States of America

99 98 97 96 95 | 8 7 6 5 4

Contents

Preface

Acting It Out is aimed at teenagers — both in groups and in classes — in schools, agencies, institutions, or churches. Its purpose is to provide, through drama and improvisational theatre, a means for resolving conflicts, for establishing high self-esteem, and for promoting acceptable behavior.

Teenagers are often reluctant to discuss serious problems that affect their own lives. With *Acting It Out*, they can express their feelings and emotions through a character. Each of the dramas is deliberately short so that it may be used in one of two ways: first, simply to stimulate discussion of a topic or issue; or second, to provide the beginning of an improvisational *scene*, in which the actor/participants continue the dialogue without the use of a printed script. A part of the plays' value is that the dramas provide a safe and secure setting for discussion, no matter what form it takes.

The idea of using drama to illustrate areas of concern certainly is not new. It has been used for years in various types of problem-solving and situations. Many books deal with psycho-drama and the use of fictional characters to help us deal with our own problems. However, *Acting It Out* is the first book to provide short plays that can be used as the basis for exploring concerns of teenagers.

The plays are arranged alphabetically according to the problems they address.

Introduction

Teenagers are a wonderful, sometimes complex, and often misunderstood generation. They have been accused of being uncommunicative and of living in a world of their own. Adults express a desire to penetrate the barrier and reach into this other world, but they do not know how and frequently feel tuned out by the teenagers.

"We need a tool that will help us get started communicating with one another," declared the mother of three teenagers. "Something that is presented in an objective way and that will enhance further discussion about special topics."

"Communication opens the door to understanding," said the peer counseling teacher of a public high school. "It would be very helpful to have a book of short dramas that would lead to an opportunity for open discussion in the group."

A church youth leader expressed a similar desire. "What I need to help me with group discussion is a springboard to get us started. We need to talk about real concerns of teenagers, but it is often difficult to find a way to get the young people to share their feelings about painful issues."

A drug counselor was explicit when he said, "If we had some open-ended dramas dealing with alcohol and drug abuse, we would find them very useful." The same feeling was echoed by a suicide prevention counselor.

The general theme was the same for all of the people who worked with youth in schools (private and public), churches, drug-rehabilitation centers and half-way houses, private homes, summer camps, retreats, suicide prevention centers, eating disorder clinics, and informal, spontaneous gatherings. They wanted a resource to use for group discussion, a helpful aid that would motivate teenagers to express their true feelings.

This book was written to fulfill that need. It offers assistance to the professional and the non-professional, the beginner and the experienced. Questions at the close of each drama are presented to provoke thought and initiate discussion.

The teenagers who will be using these dramas should be non-judgmental when listening and responding to the comments of their peers. If young people feel they will not be put down when expressing their feelings, they will be more inclined to take a risk and join the discussion. The non-judgmental, "no put down" rule may be established before the questions are read. Along the same line self-esteem is increased when people feel valued be their peer group. Encouraging words to the shy person who has spoken out for the first time since he or she joined the group will motivate him or her to speak again.

Young people may find reading a part in one of the dramas less threatening than voicing their own concerns. Hiding behind a role may result in a teenager gaining enough confidence later to step out from behind the mask and be himself or herself.

As the leader uses this book with various groups, he or she will find the dramas discussed differently at each meeting. New readers will discuss the plays from their unique points of view, which may vary greatly from the previous group's. Therefore, the plays will stay interesting for the group leader, even though he or she may hear them many times. Use this book frequently and you will find your discussions will come alive, and communication will reach a new level, which will be beneficial to both the teenager and the adult.

Both authors have a common interest: to help teenagers and the adults who work with them. This book is the result of that common interest. These dramas may be used anywhere you find teenagers, whether they are in a group setting or at home with their parents. Anyone who wants to understand teenagers better will find this book helpful.

ADOPTION

Wanting to Find Biological Parents

*The action takes place in the living room of the
McLeod house. It is Saturday morning.*
Larry *and his dad are talking.*

Larry: I wish you knew more about my parents.

Dad: Your biological parents?

Larry: Yeah, I wonder about them sometimes. I always
thought it would be nice to find them.

Dad: Why?

Larry: Curiosity mostly, I guess. I'd like to see what they're
like. How they look. What kind of people they are. (*He
looks at his dad.*) You know a little about them, though.

Dad: Just in general terms. I have the pamphlet from *Child
Services*. You've seen it. Your mother and I plan to let
you have it sometime.

Larry: How about now?

Dad: Sure. But it won't tell you a lot about your parents. (*He goes to a desk in the corner and opens a drawer. He pulls out a folder containing the pamphlet.*) Here it is. It tells where you were born, when, how much you weighed. All the usual stuff.

Larry: I remember. (*He takes the folder and glances through it.*) It says my birth parents came from neighboring towns and that they wanted to get married. Their parents wouldn't let them.

Dad: They were so young. Both fifteen, I think. Younger than you are now. Isn't that something?

Larry: Wow, I hadn't thought of that. Now they'd be what? Thirty-one?

Dad *nods.*

Larry: My birth dad was short and stocky, and my birth mom fairly short, too. I'm surprised.

Dad: I'll bet they'd be surprised to see how tall you are.

Larry: Dad, is there any way...?

Dad: We, your mom and I, were told not to try to find them. We were even told that if, somehow, they found out we had you before the adoption was final, it was possible we'd have to give you back. Your mom and I worried constantly for six months.

Larry: Would they really do that?

Dad: Maybe. Who knows? The case worker told us about an instance where the biological mother found out who had her baby, and kept demanding money.

Larry: Sometimes I worry, too.

Dad: Worry? What about, Larry?

Larry: All kinds of things. That maybe there's something wrong with my real parents that will be wrong with me. An inherited disease. Or that they have traits that aren't too good. And I'll turn out like them.

Dad: Maybe someday you can look for them.

Larry: Does that bother you, Dad?

Dad: That you want to find them?

Larry: Yes.

Dad: To be perfectly honest, I'd have to say it does. Maybe it makes me feel a little hurt. Your mom and I have done our best. We're not perfect, but we tried.

Larry: I know that. But it's something I have to do. It's like deep inside, I'm a little frightened. A little uncertain about...about who I am. About *what* I am.

Dad: I think I can understand. I suppose I'd want to know, too. But look, Larry, promise me you won't build up your hopes.

Larry: About finding them someday?

Dad: Partly that. But even more, you don't really know what to expect.

Larry: The pamphlet says both sets of grandparents were community leaders. Chances are, then...

Dad: ...that your biological parents are fine, upstanding people. I expect that they are.

Larry: I'd like to know how they feel. I'd like to know if they ever think about me. If they ever wonder about me and try to imagine how I look and what I'm like.

Dad: It must have been terribly hard. Especially for them. Especially since they did want to marry.

Larry: (*Sighs.*) I wonder if I'll ever know.

Questions for Discussion

1. What are some reasons why adopted children want to find their biological parents? What would be the reasons why some would not?

2. Discuss Larry's apparent relationship with his adoptive father. List words to describe it.

3. Discuss reasons why biological parents give up their children for adoption.

4. If a counselee asks a peer counselor to help him or her brainstorm ideas on how to look for a biological parent, what referral agencies might be suggested?

5. From a biological parent's point of view, discuss what problems might arise from a child finding that parent. Discuss what the positive outcomes might be.

Giving Up a Baby for Adoption

The action takes place in a peer counseling class.

Holly: I still think of the baby, and I wonder how it is. No, not "it." *She* — a little girl. And I wonder how she is.

Lon: I suppose it's natural. I mean, to think of her, to wonder about her.

Holly: I'm missing out on everything. I don't know what she looks like, whether she can walk and talk now. I'll bet she can.

Lon: Are you sorry you gave her up for adoption? Is that what you mean?

Holly: Yeah, I'm sorry. I'm sorry, I'm sorry.

Fay: It's OK, Holly. Maybe we can't understand exactly, but we can sympathize. It must have been a hard decision.

Holly: I could never have had an abortion. I don't think it's right. (*She looks around the classroom.*) I mean, for me it wasn't right. Maybe for someone else... But I couldn't keep the baby. I really couldn't keep her. Even though I wanted to. Even though...

Earle: You think you should have tried.

Holly: Yeah. It would have ruined my life, but that's being selfish, isn't it?

Fay: Not necessarily. The people who got her, maybe they couldn't have kids, and really wanted them. I think couples are investigated pretty thoroughly.

Holly: But you never know for sure what they're like. All those books about child abuse. Movie stars beating their kids, torturing them. Some of those kids were adopted.

Lon: But that's not a very common thing, I wouldn't think. For adoptive parents to abuse their kids. Like Fay said, don't the agencies really investigate people who want to adopt?

Holly: I suppose so. But that's not the point. I think of her every day at least a hundred times. I've even given her a name, a secret name that I call her. Laurie Lee. Dark brown hair, big brown eyes. Laurie Lee. I want to hold her. I just want to hold her once.

Fay: Holly?

Holly: Yes?

Fay: I know it must be awfully hard, but maybe you're dwelling on it too much.

Lon: It seems to me you're torturing yourself. You did what you thought was best. You examined alternatives, and then you had to choose. What if you try to think now of those other alternatives? Really think about them. You must have rejected them for a lot of reasons.

Holly: I already said...about abortion.

Lon: I know. So be proud of the fact that you gave that baby life. Can you be proud of that?

Earle: And what would have happened if you'd have kept her? Could you have finished school? Would the father have married you? You probably couldn't have gone on after high school. To college or anything.

Holly: I know. Mom said she'd take care of the baby sometimes. But that isn't fair either. She already raised her family.

Lon: So in that respect you chose the right alternative.

Holly: I know. I know all the arguments. I know a couple is better than a single parent. I know that I couldn't really afford to take care of her.

Fay: But still you can't help thinking.

Holly: Yeah.

Fay: And that's OK, isn't it? Anyone's bound to think of a child they've given up. And they're going to wonder about him or her. I think that's natural.

Holly: But I shouldn't let it take over my life. (*Pause.*) That's easy to say, but not so easy to do.

Questions for Discussion

1. Do you think that Holly believes she made the right decision?

2. What other choices did she have?

3. What would you have said to Holly?

4. Do you think she will ever work through her guilt?

5. Holly said, "It would have ruined my life, but that's being selfish, isn't it?" Do you feel she was selfish? Why or why not?

AIDS

Death from AIDS

The action takes place on the steps of the school, just after classes have been dismissed for the day.

Aileen: Wasn't that film in health class just awful?

Hope: Gruesome. When I think of all those people dying... I thought AIDS was something that happened to people you didn't know. The kind I'd never even meet.

Earl: You mean gays, don't you? Homosexuals?

Hope: And addicts, I guess. Come to think of it, I suppose there are lots of kids right here in school who are hooked on drugs.

Earl: And gay guys, too. You'd be surprised.

Aileen: (*Laughing.*) You aren't trying to tell us something, are you?

Earl: (*In a mocking voice.*) Maybe I am. Maybe I have AIDS, and I'm breathing all over you, and you'll get AIDS too.

Hope: I don't think that's funny.

Earl: You know what? Neither do I. The whole thing makes me angry.

Aileen: Anyhow, you can't get AIDS like that.

Hope: Like what?

Aileen: Like people breathing on you.

Earl: (*With tears in his eyes.*) You want to know something terrible? My brother contracted AIDS.

Hope: Are you serious?

Earl: My brother Lenny. He graduated a couple of years ago. Did either of you know him?

Both girls shake their heads.

Earl: Yeah, well, he was in college. At State. All at once he became ill. He dropped out of school and came home.

Hope: I'm sorry, Earl. I mean I'm really sorry.

Aileen: How long...?

Earl: He found out last spring. And he had to tell my parents. And can you believe it? They said they were embarrassed. They said it was the most embarrassing thing that ever happened. They didn't want him at home, and they didn't want to hear where he was or how he was doing.

Hope: They kicked him out?

Earl: Hey, you know, I always loved my brother. And they kicked him out. And I couldn't understand that. They're religious. They've always been so religious. But when it come right down to it, they weren't religious at all.

Aileen: He's...gay?

Earl: Yeah. But more important, he's a person, and my brother. He taught me how to throw a baseball, and how to ride a bike. He took me fishing and to the circus and all that kind of stuff because Mom and Dad were too busy. Too busy working and earning money and —

Aileen: Take it easy, Earl. Getting so worked up isn't going to help.

Earl: I tried to keep track. There's an AIDS foundation in town. He went to them for help. He found a place to stay. (*Closing his eyes for a moment.*) I guess that's why I acted like I did about breathing on you. I'm so angry, so frustrated. My parents told me I couldn't see him anymore.

Aileen: They were probably afraid you'd get AIDS too.

Earl: So what? (*Sighs.*) I don't mean that. I was afraid too. I thought you could get it from breathing the same air, or shaking hands or whatever. And I didn't see him for a long time. But then I did.

Hope: What did your parents say?

Earl: I didn't tell them at first. But then I tried to talk to them about all this stuff the doctors say about how AIDS is transmitted. You know, about needles and transfusions and sexual contact. They really got angry. They threatened to kick me out if I saw him again.

Aileen: Did you? See him, I mean.

Earl: Yeah, I saw him. And he wasn't like my brother at all. He was skinny and covered with purple blotches. And I couldn't stand it. Then he smiled. And he was like his old self...like he was going to get out of his bed and take me fishing again. (*Pause.*) I tried to see him every day. And other people with AIDS. People who were kicked out by their families.

Aileen: Do you mean you went to see other people, too?

Earl: All sorts. Little babies born with AIDS. Kids who are hemophiliacs and received bad blood. A woman who got AIDS through a transfusion, her husband, who got it from her. I try to see one or two of them every day.

Hope: Then your parents —

Earl: No. Just last week I moved out. I'm staying with an aunt here in town. She's a nurse. She knows.

Aileen: Your parents forced you to leave?

Earl: Sometimes I think maybe I can understand how they feel. But I've got to do what I do. My brother had no one but me. All those others have no one but me and people like me.

Hope: What do you mean?

Earl: I'm a volunteer for the AIDS Project. We need other volunteers.

Aileen: I have a part-time job...

Earl: What about you, Hope?

Hope: It's a big thing, Earl. I have to think it over.

Aileen: Hope's right.

Earl: It's just people. People not much different from you and me. All ages, all races, all types.

Hope: What about your brother?

Earl: Lenny? He died the day I moved out.

Questions for Discussion

1. According to Earl, how is AIDS transmitted? What are some of the ways it's often wrongly believed to be transmitted?

2. List some feeling words that would describe Earl when he visited his brother.

3. List some feeling words that would describe Earl's parents.

4. What are some things Earl gained by visiting his brother? What are some things he lost?

5. Discuss your feelings about people who have AIDS.

AIDS: A Family Problem

The action occurs in a peer counseling class.

Monica: I don't need help with this case, but I do need to unload.

Eric: Sounds like something heavy.

Monica: Heartbreaking would be a better word.

Lois: Did someone die? Someone close to your counselee?

Monica: No. But the pain may be just as bad. (*She looks at the other class members.*) Yesterday, a new boy on campus was sitting alone at lunchtime. He looked so sad, I decided to introduce myself and see if I could cheer him up. He seemed so glad to meet someone that I sat with him to eat.

Lois: (*Jokingly.*) And I'll bet he was cute.

Monica: He was. But believe me, he needed a peer counselor more than he needed a girlfriend.

Eric: So what was his problem?

Monica: His parents had just told him before they moved that his younger brother has AIDS.

Eric: Wow. That would be rough to hear. How old is the brother?

Monica: He's in the sixth grade, so probably eleven or twelve.

Lois: How did a young kid like that get AIDS? Not drugs.

Monica: No, he's a hemophiliac.

Lois: I can understand why the boy you met needed to talk to someone. Just being new on campus would be enough.

Monica: I asked him why the family moved. He said they wanted to be close to the medical center.

Eric: It must be awful to leave all your friends behind. Especially when you need them the most.

Monica: I got the impression there was another reason for moving.

Eric: Like what?

Monica: They're from a small town, where it's not so easy to hide as it is in a big city.

Eric: What do you mean?

Monica: You know, where you have to answer a lot of questions. Where you have to take the chance of being rejected.

Eric: Because of having AIDS in the family?

Monica: People can really be cruel to AIDS patients and their families. There's so much fear and ignorance.

Lois: I know I was afraid to be around anyone with AIDS till we learned about it in class.

Eric: How was your counselee when you left him?

Monica: He seemed glad for the opportunity to talk. I'm going to meet with him tomorrow, so he knows he's not all alone anymore on campus. He has support. I'd like for some of the rest of you to meet him too. It's going to be a long haul for him, and he's going to need all of us.

Eric: Maybe he could visit our class some time.

Monica: I've thought about asking him to sign up for it next semester. He seems like a sensitive, caring guy. I bet he'd make a great peer counselor. But I don't want to get ahead of myself. Right now he just needs support.

Questions for Discussion

1. Discuss the way Monica approached the new student. What lessons can another peer counselor learn from her?

2. Why do a higher percentage of hemophiliacs contract AIDS than other people?

3. Discuss why the parents wanted to move from their small community. Do you think prejudice against families of AIDS patients is decreasing? Why or why not?

4. How can the peer counseling class best support the new student?

CHILD ABUSE

Physical Abuse

It is just before the beginning of senior English. **Mary** *is standing at the classroom door, glancing through her notebook.* **Susie** *moves down the hallway and tries to sneak past* **Mary**. *She is ashamed and tries not to be noticed. She has a black eye, ugly welts on her face, and a badly bruised right arm that dangles at her side.*

Mary: Susie, what happened?

Susie: It's nothing.

Mary: Nothing? What do you mean, "nothing"?

Susie: I fell.

> *Another student,* **Tom**, *starts past the girls, then stops and stares.*

Tom: Man! What does the other guy look like?

Susie: (*Swallowing hard.*) What do you mean?

Tom: I mean, if you look like this, the other person —

> **Susie** *sobs and tries to brush past* **Tom**.

Tom: Hey, listen, I'm sorry. I didn't mean —

Mary: You didn't fall. Someone did this to you, didn't they?

Susie: I fell, that's all. I fell.

Tom: That looks pretty bad. You better go see the nurse.

Susie: I can't. (*Pleading.*) Don't you see? I can't. (*She begins to cry in earnest.*)

Mary: (*Putting her arm around* **Susie**'s *shoulder.*) I think I understand.

Susie: (*Jerking free.*) How can you possibly understand?

Tom: Hey, take it easy. Everything's all right.

Susie: Yeah, sure. Everything's perfect.

Mary: Who did this to you, Susie?

Susie: I don't know what you mean.

Mary: The same kind of thing happened to me. After my mom and stepdad got married, he'd get drunk. He'd get real crazy and start beating up Mom. Then he'd turn on my little brother or me. Something like that's happening to you, isn't it?

Susie: (*Giving in.*) You're right. But what am I going to do?

Mary: Does anyone know about this? Anyone else in your family?

Susie: Dad knows. He's afraid to tell anyone. He's afraid Mom will be arrested.

Tom: (*Incredulous.*) Your mother did this?

Susie: It's like she becomes a whole different person some- times. I never know when it's going to happen.

Tom: How long has this been going on?

Susie: I don't know. Maybe six months. We always got along before.

Mary: Look, Susie, this has to be reported.

Susie: I told you that my dad —

Tom: But what if it happens again?

Susie: I don't know.

Tom: It could be worse. You could be hurt bad.

Mary: Tom's right.

Susie: I wish you hadn't found out.

Mary: What about talking to one of the counselors?

Susie: If I say what happened, they have to report it. Don't they?

Mary: Yes. Yes, they do.

Susie: Well, then?

Questions for Discussion

1. What did Mary think happened to Susie? How was she able to figure this out?

2. Why did Susie lie at first about what happened to her? Why is she afraid to tell anyone the truth?

3. Do you think Tom understands the situation? How does he react to what is happening?

4. What can the others do to help Susie? How do you think she can be helped?

5. How would you react if you learned that a friend or classmate was being abused? What would you do?

6. Why do you think Susie's father is afraid to tell anyone what is happening?

Emotional Abuse

The action occurs at a fast food restaurant
where **Laura, Chad, Tina,** *and* **Josh** *have stopped*
after a movie.

Chad: That was a pretty weird movie. Can you imagine the guy going nuts like that?

Tina: Our backgrounds help mold us. We might all be different in different circumstances. I think that's the point of the film.

Chad: What about a person's character? Isn't that important?

Laura: Sure it's important, Chad. But I think what Tina means is that even if we are a particular way to begin with, our environment molds us. Like a sculptor molding a piece of clay. It starts out a certain way, but it may end up as a figure or whatever. In the end, it's still clay, but its shape is different.

Chad: A person isn't a hunk of clay. I'm supposed to believe that just because this guy's girlfriend made fun of him at a high school dance he became a killer?

Tina: Maybe not that by itself. But other things too. Negative things.

Chad: Well, maybe. (*Turns to* **Josh.**) What do you think?

Josh: I don't think I'm a very good person to ask.

Chad: Why not?

Josh: I guess I'm pretty bitter about some things that happened to me.

Chad: Really?

Josh: Let's just drop it, OK?

Tina: Maybe it'll help to talk about it.

Laura: Sure, Josh, it might. A good listener —

Josh: Oh, I get it. You two are in that class, aren't you? Peer...whatever it is.

Laura: Yes, and it's a big help. For me anyhow. Not just with specific things but with life in general. I think you become more accepting of people. At least you don't judge them as much.

Josh: What is this? Back to the '60s, with peace and love and...flower children?

Laura: Laugh if you want, but...

Josh: Well, I've always stayed away from that sort of thing. It's nobody's business how I feel or what happened to me.

Tina: Are you implying something did happen? Something you'd rather not talk about?

Josh: That's my business, isn't it?

Tina: You're right. I shouldn't butt in.

Chad: Is there something bothering you, Josh? If there is, I'd be glad to listen. That's what friends are for, right?

Josh: You people are trying to wear me down.

Chad: I just want you to know I'm here. That's it. End of subject.

Laura: Are we ready to go?

Josh: Maybe there *is* something I need to talk about.

Laura: Sure, Josh, what is it?

Josh: I understand how the guy felt, the man in the movie. I mean I really do. It's like what my parents always do to me.

Tina: What do you mean?

Josh: They always have to be right. They always have to win.

Laura: In what way?

Josh: In any argument or anything. It's like them against the world. Or at least against me.

Chad: I never knew that. I thought your parents were OK.

Josh: I know. That's what they want all my friends to think.

Laura: I still don't understand.

Josh: OK, let's take an example. We have a disagreement. Maybe I want to go out, and Mom decides I've been going out too much. I should study or do my chores. I try to explain my side of it, and Mom will hardly let me talk. She starts screaming about how terrible I am, and then

32

Dad joins in. They really come down hard. They browbeat me, you know?

Chad: My parents try to explain everything rationally and never get mad if I don't understand.

Josh: It's not like that with my mom and dad. It's like they won't stop till I admit they're right.

Laura: So what do you do?

Josh: I used to be really stubborn about it. I'd keep on arguing. But the more I argued, the worse they got. Once, Dad trashed my room. Just because I forgot to take out the garbage.

Tina: He tore your room apart?

Josh: Not at first. I told him I'd take out the trash, and he asked when. "I will," I said. "I told you I would." "Then do it," he told me. I said, "As soon as this show is over, all right?" Well, we kept on arguing, and then Mom got in on it. It ended up with Dad's saying that if I liked trash so much, he'd make trash of everything I owned.

Laura: He actually trashed your stuff?

Josh: It was like he went completely nuts. He knocked over my bookcase, threw my radio into the wall. All kinds of stuff.

Chad: I can't believe it's your father we're talking about.

Josh: But you know what? I learned that if I just say, "OK, you're right. I'll do whatever you want," there's never any arguing.

Chad: But didn't you ever try talking to them about it?

Josh: Are you kidding?

Tina: That wouldn't work, huh?

Josh: You'd better believe it.

Chad: There must be something you can do.

Josh: Yeah, sure. But what?

Questions for Discussion

1. What things other than environment make people who they are?

2. List some steps Josh could use to communicate better with his parents.

3. Were Laura, Chad, and Tina too forceful in trying to get Josh to talk about his problems? Why or why not?

4. Discuss Josh's father's action in destroying Josh's room. Why do you think he reacted in such a violent way?

5. How do you think Josh will treat his own children later on?

Witnessing Abuse

The action occurs in a classroom setting.

Kim: I need to talk about something that doesn't directly concern me, but it's pretty important. And I've got to figure out what to do. I'm not going to tell you who I'm talking about, because the situation would have to be reported if I did.

Rhea: Sounds like it involves child abuse.

Kim: That's right.

Elaine: But if someone's in trouble—some kid—don't you think you should report it?

Kim: First of all, who would listen? I'm not an adult. And this has nothing to do with my family.

Roger: Maybe we can help you figure something out.

Kim: It's a family who lives nearby. They have a son in high school and a daughter in junior high. The father and step-mother both work, so the kids are pretty much on their own. Latch-key kids, I guess.

Lionel: Are you worried because they're being neglected?

Kim: Partly.

Lionel: What else?

Kim: I can look out my bedroom window and see across to this house. One day the girl came home and couldn't get in. Her brother wasn't home yet. She finally got so mad she kicked the storm door and broke the glass.

Rhea: What did her parents do?

Kim: That's the whole thing. I found out later she lied and told them the glass was already broken, that apparently someone had tried to get into the house. A burglar.

Elaine: And then I'll bet her parents found out that she lied.

Kim: They called the police, and the police discovered the girl's shoeprint on the broken glass.

Lionel: And she was in big trouble, right?

Kim: For hours I heard screaming and noises like things being thrown.

Elaine: Did you find out what it was?

Kim: Yeah, I did. And I couldn't believe it.

Roger: What did they do?

Kim: I saw the girl the next day. She was covered with bruises. But worst of all, her hand was terribly burned.

Rhea: The parents did that? They scalded her hand?

Kim: Yes. And a lot of other things, too. Like I said, the screaming had gone on for hours. The girl told me the noises I heard were when she was slammed over and over again into the walls. She got away and tried to lock herself inside the bathroom. Her father slammed open the door. She was squeezed up against the bathtub, squatting down. He grabbed her and started to shake her. Each time he did, her head hit the tub.

Elaine: You've got to report them. You just have to.

Kim: I talked to my Mom and Dad, and they seemed to think it was too late. I don't know.

Lionel: You said she was scalded.

Kim: Her stepmother did it. She turned on the water as hot as she could in the bathroom sink. Then she held Deena's hands underneath. Over and over again, all the time screaming at her about how this would teach her a lesson.

Elaine: Deena? I know who that is. They're friends of my family. I knew they lived on your street —

Kim: I didn't want you to know who it is. I don't know what to do.

Rhea: You have to report them. You or your parents.

Kim: That was a couple of weeks ago. No one would believe me.

Lionel: Someone has to believe you. The next time could be worse.

Kim: Her brother graduates this year. He has a good job already. He says he's going to move out and take Deena with him.

Lionel: Are you willing to take the chance that nothing will happen before that? That her parents won't do something else?

Questions for Discussion

1. Should abuse be reported even if several weeks have passed since the incident occurred?

2. What do you think Kim should do?

3. Name the people you think the girl came into contact with who probably saw the bruises and the evidence of scalding. What are some reasons they would not have reported it? By law, teachers must report suspicion of child abuse. Do you think her teacher did or did not report it?

4. Kim's stepmother said she was teaching Kim a lesson. What do you think are effective methods parents can use to discipline their children?

5. Child abusers themselves have often been abused as children. Discuss ways these cycles can be broken.

Sexual Abuse 1

The setting is a peer counseling class.

Barbara: Anyhow, I hate my father for what he did. But I still love him. It's all mixed up.

Tony: You've never talked to anyone about this before?

Barbara: I was ashamed and guilty. It's like it's my fault, somehow.

Dixie: What do you mean?

Barbara: I was thirteen when it started, so I knew about...about that kind of thing. It was two days after my birthday. Mom had gone shopping and taken my little brother. (*Her voice breaks.*)

Tony: Look, Barb, we know how tough this is to talk about. But it helps. It sure helped me.

Dixie: We're with you, Barb, you know that.

Barbara: (*Glancing from one to the other, tears in her eyes.*) But it's always been this deep, dark secret. At first, Dad pretended it was a game. Our very own game that we wouldn't share with anyone. I... I guess I knew it was really wrong. But I listened to my dad. You're supposed to listen to your dad, aren't you?

Ed: What no one tells you is that your parents aren't always right. No one is. Parents, teachers, religious leaders. They make mistakes or do things they know are wrong. Everyone does.

Barbara: That's no excuse! Not for what my father started that day.

Ed: What I meant was that we're taught to listen to our elders. And when we're young, we do this blindly. (*He shrugs.*) Or at least we think we should, even though we sometimes don't. You were at the age when you still trusted your father completely. You looked to him for...I don't know, for guidance, for how to live.

Barbara: Then why did I feel so guilty? And later so cheap? (*She cries softly.*) Like a...like a hooker or something. I was only thirteen.

Dixie: You mean then this wasn't a one-time thing?

Barbara: It went on and on and on.

Tony: (*Very gently.*) Barb?

Barbara: Yes?

Tony: Is he still... I mean, does your father...?

Barbara: (*Crying out.*) I can't say any more about it. I can't. I'm all mixed up. I wouldn't want to get him into trouble.

Dixie: What do you mean?

Barbara: You know the laws. We've talked about them. Any time a teacher or someone hears about this kind of thing, they have to report it. I can just see what would happen. It would kill my mom.

Ed: Your mother doesn't know? She doesn't suspect?

Barbara: Maybe she suspects. You've got to understand my mom. I suppose...I suppose you'd call her old-fashioned. Very religious. What her husband says is right.

Tony: But you've got to think about you.

Barbara: I know. I don't know what to do. And, yes, Tony, to answer your question, every time Mom is gone... When I know she's going shopping or something, I try to go along. Ever since the first few times, I've tried to avoid being alone with Dad. But sometimes I don't realize she's gone. Sometimes, it's at night, and there's nowhere I can go.

Dixie: Look, Barbara, any time you need to, you can come to my house. OK? We don't live that far apart. If you need a ride, my mom and dad can pick you up.

Barbara: Thanks, Dixie. I appreciate it. I'll keep that in mind.

Ed: Your home life must be awful.

Barbara: I realize this is probably hard to understand. But in a lot of ways, my dad's a nice man. He works hard. He's an attorney. Sometimes he even takes cases for free, when people can't afford a lawyer and he feels their rights are being violated.

Tony: That makes it even harder, doesn't it?

Barbara: He's always taken time to help my brother and me with problems, to explain homework we didn't understand. (*Pause.*) In spite of what he's done, I guess...I guess I really love him. And that must make me some kind of freak.

Ed: No, Barb. Don't ever think that. Maybe I can understand. It's just one facet of the man. The bad part. It's a pretty terrible part, I realize, but still, it isn't the total person.

Barbara: So, what am I going to do?

Tony: The situation's serious. This — what he did, what he does — is an ongoing thing.

Barbara: At first, it was so innocent. He said his back was hurting, and asked me to rub it. I did, and then he said it was my turn. He rubbed my back and then he pulled me close and gave me a kiss. (*She stops.*) I don't think I can say this.

Ed: Maybe the details don't matter. We understand.

Barbara: I should have suspected, but I didn't. Looking back, I see that he started paying a lot more attention to me six months or so before this happened. He was always a loving man with Mom and Peter and me. But when he kissed me, it was just a little too long. When he hugged me, I'd start to feel uncomfortable and try to pull away. But he acted hurt, so I didn't make a big deal out of it.

Dixie: Look, Barbara, someone's going to have to report this. You realize that, don't you?

Barbara: I know. But then what? What's going to happen to my family?

Questions for Discussion

1. Discuss Barbara's statement, "I hate my father for what he did, and yet I still love him." Do you think that it's possible to feel both emotions about a person?

2. Why do you think Barbara shares her story with the peer counseling class?

3. Barbara says she doesn't want to cause any trouble for her father. Does she know that the teacher must report it if Barbara talks about it in class?

4. Why do you think fathers abuse their daughters?

5. Why do you think Barbara doesn't talk to her mother about the abuse?

6. Name people or agencies Barbara could have gone to earlier for help.

Sexual Abuse 2

The action occurs in the high school courtyard, just
after a peer counseling session. **Alan** *and* **Ross** *are*
leaning against the wall, talking with **Penny** *and* **Kay**.

Alan: Well, I certainly understand how Virginia feels about her parents, the way she was talking about them in peer counseling.

Ross: What do you mean?

Alan: I hate my father, too. I totally hate him. You know, sometimes I lie in bed at night, thinking of ways to kill him.

Kay: Your father must have done some pretty awful things.

Alan: You could say that.

Penny: Do you want to tell us? Or maybe bring it up in class?

Alan: I've never talked to anyone about it. Except my brother. Once a neighbor came and tried to talk to Mom about...about what Dad was doing, about something she

44

saw him do. But Mom wouldn't listen. It's like she's denying the whole thing.

Kay: You've never had anyone you could go to?

Alan: I don't think most people would believe me. My father's very active in civic organizations. I don't think anyone suspects what he's really like.

Ross: What is he like, Alan?

Alan: I'm not sure I can talk about this. I'm not sure I even want to. Sometimes, in class, I think how great it would be to get it into the open. Just to tell people how I feel. But then I wonder what good it really would do.

Penny: Remember when we talked about my problems? The drugs, I mean.

Alan: Yeah. Sure, I remember. I admired you for talking about it. And even more for taking a step in the right direction.

Penny: Once I got it into the open, I realized I had to do something about it. It was like saying, "Now it's here and everyone knows. So I can't pretend anymore."

Alan: I guess. (*He sighs.*) You'll think I'm crazy, but when I was a little kid—six, seven—I'd get so frustrated over how my father treated me, that I'd go outside and pound my head against the side of the house.

Ross: It must have been bad.

Alan: It was the beatings. Dad whipped me and slammed me around. He had this old leather belt. He'd make me get undressed—

Kay: Your mother ignored this? She didn't do anything?

Alan: Once. It was over some dumb thing, some little thing. I'd disagreed with my grandfather about something. Mom's dad, I mean. And my dad started yelling about how I should respect my elders. I tried to tell him it was nothing. I wasn't mad at Grandpa or anything. It was more like a...like a debate, maybe. Dad grabbed hold of me and yanked me into another room. And then he went completely nuts.

Ross: What did he do?

Alan: There was that look in his eye. Like he was getting really excited. Like it was a real turn-on. He grabbed me around the neck and started to squeeze. I couldn't breathe and was starting to black out, and he kept pounding my head into the wall, harder and harder. I really thought he was going to kill me.

Kay: What did you do?

Alan: I couldn't do anything. He was bigger, and besides, he was my father.

Ross: What happened?

Alan: Mom came running down the steps screaming for him to stop, that he was going to kill me. She grabbed his arm and tried to pull him away. Suddenly, he let go and left for work. He worked at night. I wanted to leave. I wanted to run away and never come back.

Kay: Is this kind of thing still happening?

Alan: Yeah, well, not like that. He still goes a little crazy sometimes—

Kay: What about your mother? Did she ever try to stop him again?

Alan: That was the only time. And I felt like I wanted to die. I just wanted to die. I was in the choir at church, and that night we were going to go Christmas caroling. Dad was supposed to have taken me, before all that happened. So, I decided to walk. I knew I'd never make it in time. It was about ten miles. But I had to get away, maybe permanently. I was walking along a highway outside of town, and I decided, "This is it." There weren't any cars coming. I walked to the middle of the road, lay down, and closed my eyes, bracing myself. Telling myself it would soon be over.

Penny: That's awful.

Alan: But there weren't any cars. A busy highway, and no cars. And I started to shiver so hard my whole body shook. So I stood up and kept on walking.

Ross: What about later?

Alan: Life just went on. I tried to avoid my dad as much as I could. You know, the worst thing, the thing that made me feel the worst, was that some time, I don't remember exactly when, I realized my dad was really getting turned on sexually by what he was doing.

Ross: Maybe now I can understand a little about your feelings. About hating your dad.

Alan: When I leave home—when I'm eighteen, I mean—I never want to see him again.

Kay: But you're not eighteen yet.

Alan: No. I'm not eighteen.

Ross: So what are you going to do till then?

Questions for Discussion

1. Are Ross, Penny, and Kay required to report Alan's abuse?

2. Why do you think Alan's mother never did anything to help her son?

3. Discuss Alan's actions when he lay down in the middle of the road. Describe how you think he must have been feeling.

4. With the information you have and your own imagination, make a profile of Alan's father. Do you know other people who fit this profile?

5. Make a profile of Alan's mother. List ways she could change her situation.

Sexual Abuse 3

The action takes place in a peer counseling setting.

Rob: Yesterday Barbara was talking about things that happened with her father. I... I didn't have anything happen with my family, but there *is* something that's bothered me for years.

Lou: Does this have something to do with sexual abuse?

Rob: Most of the time, I don't think about it. I try not to, anyhow. It happened so long ago.

Holly: It seems to me that it must still be bothering you. Right?

Rob: I tried to talk to my mother about it, but she said I should just forget it. It was like she wanted to push the whole thing away. She said not to tell my dad, or he'd really be angry.

Melody: What is it, Rob? What happened?

Rob: I guess I was about eleven or twelve. Just starting to know about sex. Just becoming interested, I guess. I went to this movie—it was a double feature, Saturday afternoon. I liked to sit in the back, where there weren't so many kids. I liked to be by myself to enjoy the picture. (*He pauses.*) This is really embarrassing. Barbara mentioned being ashamed. I guess I am, too.

Lou: Are you saying that something happened to make you ashamed?

Rob: (*Protesting.*) No! (*He sighs.*) It wasn't my fault. It really wasn't my fault.

Melody: Do you want to tell us about it?

Rob: I was sitting there, really into the film—one of the *Star Trek* sequels—and this guy sat down next to me. Back then, I thought, "An old guy." But I suppose he was in his forties. "Hi, kid," he said. "Hi," I answered, without really looking. "Mind if I sit beside you?" he asked. I told him I didn't. (*He looks around the room.*) You know, I think I'd like to just forget this.

Holly: If you want to. But it seems this is really important to you. You can trust the class. You know that. It won't go beyond the walls of this room.

Rob: But all you guys are going to know.

Lou: Look, Rob, it's up to you. But maybe it will help to get it out. To be able to talk about it.

Rob: Yeah. But...but you don't understand. What the guy did wasn't so bad, I guess. But you see... You see, I really liked what he did. Don't you understand? I liked it.

Holly: You were just a kid. He was an adult.

Rob: But... I didn't want him to stop. And even though I was ashamed and guilty, there was this big thrill, too, when I'd think about it. I'm a terrible person, don't you see? I think I'm a terrible person.

Lou: Because part of you liked what was happening?

Rob: Yeah. He... He reached over and started to run his hand up and down my thigh. "Do you mind?" he asked. I was scared, but I didn't want him to stop, even though I knew it was wrong.

Holly: I think you're being too hard on yourself, Rob. I'm sure everyone has feelings like that.

Rob: I don't know. All I know is that I let the guy run his hand up and down and then... He felt up higher, and pretty soon he had my belt undone. And then he wanted me to touch him, and I did. And it was like I was doing something really dangerous, but it was exciting. And then, pretty soon, he got up and left.

Lou: That's it? That's all that happened?

Rob: Yes. No. That isn't the worst part. I went back to that movie theatre. Every time I could. Every weekend. I pretended it was just to see the film. But it wasn't. Deep down inside, I knew what I was doing. I was looking for him. Looking for that man.

Melody: That's why you feel so guilty?

Rob: I'd heard about guys who...who like boys. Who want sex with them. I'd been warned. But he seemed like a nice guy. Warm and gentle. Friendly. For those few minutes, it was like he cared about me.

Lou: So you went back looking for him? Did you ever find him again?

Rob: No, I never did.

Melody: Did the same thing ever happen again? The same kind of thing. With someone else?

Rob: No, that was the only time. And I felt so guilty I finally told my mother.

Holly: It wasn't really your fault, was it? You didn't look for it to happen.

Rob: Not that first time, no. But afterwards... I wanted to find the man again.

Lou: You had doubts about yourself. About your sexuality. Particularly since you wanted to repeat what happened.

Rob: Right. That's it.

Questions for Discussion

1. Why does Rob have doubts about his own sexuality?

2. Do you think Rob's encounter with the man in the theatre is a common problem for many young people today?

3. What other action could Rob have taken in the movie?

4. If the man had asked Rob to leave the theatre with him, do you think Rob would have gone? Why or why not?

5. Was Rob being naive in looking for the man again? What danger was avoided by Rob's not finding the man?

6. Why is Rob finding it difficult to forgive himself?

COMMUNICATION

Lack of Communication

Scene i

The action takes place in Mr. Schmidt's study. As the lights come up, **Doreen** *arrives home from school and passes the study door. She looks inside where her father is working at his desk.*

Doreen: Hi, Daddy.

Dad: (*Looking up quickly and then down at his papers once more.*) Ummm.

Doreen: (*Lightly.*) It's your daughter home from school. Can't you say "hi"?

Dad: (*Barely acknowledging her.*) Uh-huh.

Doreen: (*Entering the study.*) Can I talk to you for a minute?

Dad: I'm sorry, honey, I'm busy.

Doreen: It'll only take a minute.

Dad: Look, Doreen, you've been told a thousand times not to interrupt me when I'm working. I have to get this report done.

Doreen: Yeah, sure.

Dad: Darn it, Doreen! You know my study's off limits when I'm working.

Doreen *turns and starts to leave.*

Dad: All right. Since I'm obviously not going to get any work done, you might as well tell me what you want.

Doreen: (*Turning back to him.*) Nothing.

Dad: Yeah, just what I figured.

Doreen: Nothing I have to say ever is important, is it? I don't have any problems. I'm just a kid. Kids don't have problems. (*She storms off.*)

The lights fade.

Scene ii

The lights come up in the kitchen. **Mrs. Schmidt** *is at the sink, preparing vegetables for dinner.*

Doreen: (*Enters from the hallway.*) Mom, can I talk to you a minute?

Mom: Oh, hi, Doreen. I didn't hear you come in.

Doreen: It's really important. You see —

Mom: Now that you're here, would you please set the table?

Doreen: Listen, Mom, I got myself involved in something, and I don't know what to do.

Mom: Oh, would you please use the good set of dishes? Aunt Thelma and Uncle Claude are coming. Thelma's birthday's tomorrow, and —

Doreen: Mom, will you please listen? Please!

Mom: (*Turning to* **Doreen**.) Yes, dear, what is it?

Doreen: I'm trying to tell you, Mom. Annmarie and I accidentally found out that —

Mom: Oh, and the good silverware too, all right? You know where it is, don't you?

Doreen: (*Resigned.*) Yeah, sure, I know where it is.

The lights fade to black.

Scene iii

The lights come up in the hallway at school.

Annmarie: So, did you talk to your parents?

Doreen: Are you kidding?

Annmarie: What do you mean?

Doreen: I tried. Dad practically threw me out of his study, and all Mom wanted to talk about was setting the table to look nice for my Aunt Thelma. How about you?

Annmarie: Daddy was at a meeting, and it was Mom's night to host her book study group. I didn't get anywhere.

Doreen: You too, huh?

56

Questions for Discussion

1. Why doesn't Doreen talk to her father after he stops his work?

2. What could Doreen do differently when she asks her mother to listen?

3. Do you think most parents listen to what their kids have to say?

4. When do you find talking to your parents to be most rewarding? Consider the time of day and the circumstances. Share your thoughts with others in the class and compare for similarities.

5. Are there times when you don't listen to your parents?

Poor Communication

The action takes place in a peer counseling class.

Tammy: I want to have a deeper relationship with my boyfriend. I need help on how to do it.

Wayne: Are you talking about wanting a sexual relationship?

Tammy: Not at all. I just want us to understand each other better and to share our feelings.

Sam: Does Jack feel the same way? I mean, does he want this kind of relationship too?

Tammy: That's part of the problem. I can't communicate well enough with him to find out how he feels about anything.

Valerie: But you two have been going together for six months at least. I thought you got along really well.

Tammy: We do. We have a great time together. He's a lot of fun to be with, always laughing and joking. But the relationship's so superficial.

Sam: How do you mean?

Tammy: We're always on the go — usually with another couple or a group. We seldom have time by ourselves just to sit and talk.

Valerie: Have you planned an evening just staying at home by yourselves — maybe renting a video?

Tammy: I did even better than that. I invited him over simply to talk.

Valerie: And?

Tammy: It didn't go so well. After awhile, I tried to bring the conversation around to feelings. Serious things.

Sam: Knowing Jack as well as I do, I'll bet he tried to avoid that kind of thing.

Tammy: You're absolutely right. He kept making jokes. Then he started talking about the World Series. Not how he felt, but batting averages and that kind of thing.

Wayne: Is that the only time you tried?

Tammy: (*Sighs.*) One time in a dozen. I don't give up that easily when someone like Jack's involved. He's definitely worth working on.

Sam: Tell us about another time.

Tammy: We had a date the Friday the roles for the play were posted. I was really depressed. I'd counted on getting the lead. When I saw who got it, I wanted to cry. It wouldn't have been so bad to have lost to someone with talent. But to lose to the teacher's pet was really depressing.

Sam: And you tried to talk to Jack about it.

Tammy: Yes. I really needed someone to talk to. Don't get me wrong. It's not that he doesn't listen. He does, for a short time. Then he wants to *fix* the problem, even though that's impossible.

Sam: He's an action person. A doer. Not coming up with a solution would be really frustrating to him.

Tammy: You seem to know Jack very well. I didn't know you were friends.

Sam: "Acquaintances" would be a better word.

Tammy: I don't understand. How can you know him so well without being friends?

Sam: To be perfectly honest, I found I couldn't continue our friendship for the same reasons you're talking about.

Tammy: You used to be friends, then?

Sam: He lives a couple of blocks from my house. When he moved in, I took it upon myself to welcome him to the neighborhood. It was easy to like him, and I enjoyed introducing him around.

Wayne: I remember your bringing him to the ski club meeting.

Sam: I thought we'd become good friends, but —

Tammy: But what? Can you tell me?

Sam: There's nothing to tell. Jack just doesn't seem to want a best friend. I think it's hard for him to get close to anyone, to reveal too much of himself.

Tammy: I'm finding the same thing. It's like he's afraid to let himself like me too much.

Wayne: Could it be he's been hurt, and he's afraid to take chances again?

Sam: I wondered about that myself. On the other hand, maybe he's just a private person.

Tammy: Or maybe he just needs time. Maybe he needs someone to be patient and understanding. I wonder if I can bring him around.

Questions for Discussion

1. What might be some reasons why Jack won't let anyone get to know him well?

2. Is Tammy expecting too much by hoping Jack will change? Why or why not?

3. Why do you think Sam and Jack didn't become friends?

4. Discuss ways to help Jack learn to communicate better?

5. Should Jack be invited to join the peer counseling class? Why or why not?

DATING

Choosing a Boyfriend

The action takes place in Jan's living room. Her father is reading the paper while her mother watches TV. **Jan** *enters the room.*

Mom: (*Glancing up at* **Jan**.) Did you bring the dishes out of your room, like I asked?

Jan: (*Flaring up.*) I'll bring them out. I said I would.

Mom: When?

Jan: I said I'd bring them out. Isn't that good enough?

Dad: What's wrong with you, Jan? Your mother asked you a simple question.

Jan: Why are you always yelling at me? Why can't you leave me alone?

Mom: What is it, Jan? What's wrong?

Jan: Nothing's wrong. I just want to be left alone, that's all. I can't stand people anymore.

Dad: What happened? Did something happen?

Jan: (*Starting to cry.*) People bug me.

Mom: What people, honey?

Jan: Somebody called this morning and told me all kinds of things.

Dad: (*Laying down his paper.*) What about?

Jan: Why don't people mind their own business? There's never anyone I can trust. You think people are your friends, and they aren't.

Dad: What do you mean?

Jan: This girl, Stephanie, who's supposed to be my friend. She called and told me all kinds of things she heard about Ben. That he was out with some other girl. Then this girl I don't even know calls and tells me she wants her sweatshirt back.

Mom: What sweatshirt?

Jan: The one I'm wearing. A couple of nights ago, I told Ben I was cold, and he let me wear it. Well, this girl, Bobbie, said it was hers, that she'd given it to Ben, and she wanted it back.

Dad: What does that mean?

Jan: Don't you understand? He's supposed to be my boyfriend. And I find out he's spending time with someone else. Even worse than that, he spent the night with her. I don't like that, you know.

Dad: Did you talk to Ben about it?

Jan: We had a fight.

Mom: Did you ask him about this other girl?

Jan: No, I didn't ask him. But it must be true. Otherwise, why would he have her sweatshirt? And why would Stephanie call?

Dad: Maybe you're jumping to conclusions.

Jan: I don't think so. Ben is just like Trent. If I'd known that, I might as well have stayed with Trent.

Dad: I can't control who you see when you're not here. But that boy is forbidden from coming here again.

Jan: Oh, Dad, I'm not going to see him. I didn't mean that.

Mom: So what are you going to do? Do you think it might be a good idea to talk to Ben? He seems like a nice person.

Jan: Stephanie told me Ben spent the whole night at Bobbie's house when her parents were gone.

Dad: If he did, of course, I understand your feelings. I'd be hurt too. And angry. I'd feel betrayed. But you don't know that it's true. Not really. I think before you jump to conclusions you should talk to Ben. Without losing your temper.

Jan: I don't know if I want to.

Mom: Aw, Jan.

Jan: What? You think this isn't important because I'm just a kid. That I don't have problems.

Mom: I don't think that at all.

Jan: You know what Trent was like. Always breaking dates. Running around with other girls. Geez, Mom, he got that girl pregnant. Now it's the same thing with Ben. What's wrong with me? Why do I always pick people like that? There must be something wrong with me.

Questions for Discussion

1. Jan says, "What's wrong with me? Why do I always pick people like that?" Discuss why you believe certain people choose the wrong dates and later the wrong life partners.

2. Jan lashes out at her parents when actually she is angry at Ben. Discuss misplaced anger and its affect on people.

3. Why do you think Stephanie told Jan about Ben? Would a good friend tell?

4. Do you agree with Jan's mother that Jan should allow Ben to explain? Why or why not?

5. Why do you think Bobbie asked Jan to return the sweat-shirt instead of asking Ben for it back?

Age Difference

Scene i

The setting is the living room of the Penner house. It is early evening. **Scott** *and his mother are in the living room.*

Mom: I hope you know what you're doing.

Scott: Come on, Mom.

Mom: I don't understand what a twenty-six-year-old woman sees in a seventeen-year-old boy. What does she want from you?

Scott: We're friends, Mom, that's all.

Mom: I'd think Yvette would want friends her own age. Is something wrong with her that she can't relate to men her own age?

Scott: I told you, we're friends. I like to be with her. We enjoy each other's company.

Mom: And I suppose it was all innocent the night your car broke down and you spent the night at her apartment.

Scott: Are you asking if I'm a virgin, Mom? All right, I'm a virgin. Is that what you wanted to hear?

Mom: A twenty-six-year-old woman isn't going to be content with that for long. I think you're playing with fire.

Scott: Can't you just accept her like you accept my other friends?

Mom: You'd better think through what you're doing. I'm not going to say you can't see her. You're mature enough to make your own decisions. But for the record, I don't like the situation.

There is a knock at the door. **Scott** *answers it, and admits* **Yvette***.*

Scott: Hi, how are you doing?

Yvette: Great, how about you?

Scott: Are you ready to go?

Yvette: Sure, just let me say hi to Janet.

Mom: (*Coolly.*) Hello, Yvette.

Yvette: It's a beautiful day, isn't it? It'll be great for the concert. Did Scott tell you we're going to the outdoor theatre at State? There's a new rock group. They're supposed to be pretty good.

Mom: He told me.

Yvette: Well, so long.

Scott: 'Bye, Mom.

Blackout.

Scene ii

The lights come up on **Scott** *and* **Yvette** *sitting among a group of people on outdoor theatre bleachers.*

Scott: I can't believe my mom.

Yvette: What did she do?

Scott: You saw how she was.

Yvette: She acted a little cool toward me, that's all. Maybe she just doesn't want to let go of her son. I suppose it's hard for parents to admit their kids are growing up. I think it would be for me.

Scott: You're a very understanding woman.

Yvette: With the accent on *woman*, right?

Blackout.

Scene iii

The lights come up on a peer counseling session.

Scott: I don't understand it. My mom's never objected to anyone else I've dated. What's wrong with Yvette?

Una: Well, I know my mom and dad certainly would put their foot down if I brought home a man that age.

Scott: But why? Just because they're older doesn't mean they're monsters or anything.

Wendell: (*Laughs.*) It has to do with innocence, Peter Pan, and Never Never Land.

Scott: You'll have to explain that one, Wendell.

Wendell: Well, people in their twenties are what my mom would call *experienced*. They've been around. They know the score. So if we spend time with them, we'll become too worldly too fast. I think that's the argument.

Scott: In other words, Yvette will corrupt me?

Wendell: What do you think?

Scott: What do I think? Like I told my Mom, we enjoy each other's company. No big deal. It's not a sex thing. I don't mean I'm not attracted to Yvette. I am, and maybe she's attracted to me. But it's not going to happen. Nothing's going to happen.

Una: How can you be so sure?

Scott: I... I...

Una: I'm not saying your mother's right. But maybe you should think about the situation. Why do you and Yvette see each other? Why aren't you interested in people your own ages?

Scott: We are. I have lots of friends —

Una: That's not what I mean. There has to be a reason, maybe a number of reasons that you two have gotten together. What if you try to figure out what they are? So you understand it yourself. So you can explain it to your mother.

Scott: You think it's wrong for people of different ages to be friends?

Wendell: Or course, it isn't wrong.

Scott: Then why all this fuss about Yvette and me?

Questions for Discussion

1. Discuss the pros and cons of dating a person who is older.

2. How many years difference in age do you think is acceptable?

3. Why do you think parents are concerned when their sons or daughters date older people?

4. Why do you think Yvette would want to date a high school boy?

5. Scott told Yvette and the peer counseling class about his mother's concerns. Do you think he was looking for approval from the class, or was he having doubts himself?

Moving Away

Scene i

The action occurs in the Dobson's living room, which is cluttered with half-packed boxes. **Cassie** *sits on the arm of a chair.* **Clay** *stands near the doorway.*

Clay: Cassie, what's going on?

Cassie: We're moving.

Clay: (*Hurt.*) Why didn't you tell me?

Cassie: I just found out this morning. It's all so sudden.

Clay: Where are you going?

Cassie: You know my dad lost his job.

Clay: Yes.

Cassie: My uncle called and asked him to run one of his little markets. And my dad's afraid not to take it, with the three of us kids still in school. Oh, Clay. I don't want to go. I don't. I'll miss you and everyone else.

Clay: Can't you stay with someone here till after graduation?

Cassie: Who? I don't have any relatives here. And besides, I'll probably have to help out at the market.

Clay: Where are you moving?

Cassie: Out of state, Clay. A couple hundred miles.

Clay: When?

Cassie: This weekend. I'd give almost anything if...if we didn't have to go.

Clay: I knew that someday we'd have to go our separate ways. But not so soon.

Cassie: Promise me you'll write, OK?

Clay: Of course. And give me your phone number, too.

Cassie: Sure.

Clay: (*Pursing his lips.*) Remember Joe Newton?

Cassie: He was in the debate club, wasn't he?

Clay: Yeah.

Cassie: A good friend of yours. If I remember, you two were inseparable your sophomore year.

Clay: That's right. Before you and I started going steady.

Cassie: What about him?

Clay: He moved too. We said we'd keep in touch. We meant to. We thought we would. (*He sighs.*) I haven't heard from him in almost a year.

Cassie: But with us it'll be different.

Clay: Will it?

Cassie: Maybe this summer you can take the train to see me. Or maybe Mom will let me come back here.

The lights fade to black.

Scene ii

The lights come up. **Clay** *is sitting on the step in front of the school.*

Clay: (*Reading a letter.*) "I find I like it here OK, even though everything's different. It's a small town and a little school. Everyone knows everyone else. At first, I worried about fitting in. About making friends. (*He crumples up the letter and jams it into his pocket.*)

Lowell: (*Coming out the front door.*) What's up?

Clay: I just got a letter from Cassie.

Lowell: Your girl? The one who moved?

Clay: Right.

Lowell: What about it?

Clay: Nothing. I'm just being selfish, I guess. She likes the town and the school. She's made a lot of friends.

Lowell: That's good, isn't it?

Clay: Yeah, that's good.

The lights fade to black.

Scene iii

The lights come up on the front entrance of another school. **Cassie** *and* **Verna** *are talking.*

Verna: You look down. Do you miss your old school?

Cassie: (*Nods.*) Don't get me wrong. I like it here, but some-times...

Verna: I know. When my family moved here, I felt the same. It gets better, believe me. I don't think of my old school that much anymore.

Cassie: By the way, I just heard George Wilson asked you to the prom.

Verna: He sure did.

Cassie: That's great. The best-looking guy in the senior class.

Verna: Well, I don't like to brag. (*She laughs.*) How about you? I hear someone is interested in taking you, too.

Cassie: I've heard rumors to that effect. (*Stops and turns to* **Verna**.) I don't know what to do. Clay and I still write every day and talk every couple of weeks. But it's like we're growing distant. It's like he's only a memory.

Questions for Discussion

1. Why does a long distance relationship sometimes fade away?

2. Discuss the feelings that arise when a student changes from one school to another.

3. What would have been the pros and cons if Cassie had stayed with friends and remained in her original school till graduation?

4. Does Clay have reason to think that he and Cassie will not remain close friends after she moves away? Why or why not?

5. What can a person do to keep a friend from becoming "only a memory"?

Sneaking Dates

Scene i

The action takes place in the dining room of the Stewart house, just as **Mr. and Mrs. Stewart** *and* **Joyce** *are finishing dinner.*

Joyce: (*Laying down her napkin.*) Excuse me, please.

Dad: Where are you going?

Joyce: I... Just to a movie.

Mom: What are you going to see?

Joyce: I'm not sure. We haven't decided yet.

Dad: Who's "we"?

Joyce: Me and Reuben.

Dad: No, Joyce you're not going to do that.

Joyce: What do you mean?

Dad: I've never done this before. I've never even considered it. But I absolutely forbid you to see that boy anymore. I don't want him ever to come to this house again.

Joyce: That's not fair.

Mom: I don't understand you, Joyce. After the things you told us about him. Why would you even want to see him?

Joyce: I just do, that's all.

Dad: Look, Joyce, I'm tired of hearing you cry all the time.

Joyce: What do you mean?

Dad: You know what I mean.

Mom: We can hear you, dear. It's not that we eavesdrop, but your bedroom is next to ours. We hear you on the phone.

Joyce: You have no right.

Mom: I don't understand why you like him. He's done all sorts of things.

Joyce: Like what?

Dad: Let's start with the names.

Joyce: (*Defiantly.*) What names?

Mom: We only want what's best for you. We love you, Joyce. Don't you know that?

Joyce: And loving me means telling me who I *can* see and who I *can't*?

Dad: You know that's not true. This is the first—

Joyce: It isn't true? You mean you didn't tell me I couldn't see Reuben?

Mom: There's no need to be sarcastic, Joyce.

Joyce: So he called me some names. So what?

Mom: If it didn't bother you, you wouldn't have told us.

Dad: If anyone called your mother names like that, I'd beat him within an inch of his life.

Joyce: And you mean that's what you'll do to Reuben, too?

Dad: No, that isn't what I mean, and you know it.

Mom: Look, Joyce, you've told us how Reuben stands you up all the time.

Joyce: I know that, Mom.

Dad: Well, regardless, he's not to come here again. I don't want you to see him anymore. Is that understood?

The lights fade to black.

Scene ii

*The action occurs in a shopping mall. When the lights come up, **Joyce** and **Reuben** are sitting on a bench in front of a clothing store.*

Joyce: Anyway, you can't come to my house anymore.

Reuben: You're going to let your parents tell you what to do?

Joyce: I didn't say that, Reuben.

Reuben: Sounds like it to me.

Joyce: We can still see each other.

Reuben: But not at your house. Your parents think you're too good for me. Is that it?

Joyce: (*Sighs.*) Reuben, they can't help but know the times we were going to go somewhere and you didn't show up.

Reuben: Are you blaming me? Because if you are...

Joyce: I'm just trying to explain.

Reuben: ...because if you are, who needs it? Who needs you?

The lights fade.

Scene iii

The action takes place in a peer counseling class. When the lights come up, Joyce is talking about her relationship with Reuben and with her parents.

Joyce: I don't know what's wrong with me. I really don't. I know what kind of person he is, but I can't stay away from him. That makes me as bad as he is.

Link: Is that what you really think?

Joyce: What do you mean?

Link: Is that what you really think of yourself?

Barri: What Link means, I think, is that you don't seem to have a very high opinion of yourself.

Joyce: It's like I'm really dependent on him. If he and I are going together, everything's OK.

Link: You're still seeing each other, then?

Joyce: Yes.

Barri: What about your parents?

Joyce: (*Shaking her head.*) They don't know. They don't realize what I'm doing.

Will: What do you mean?

Joyce: Easy. I say I'm going to the library, or to a movie with a girlfriend. They don't suspect.

Link: How do you feel about all this?

Joyce: I don't know how I feel. I guess pretty rotten. I know my parents are right. I shouldn't keep on seeing this guy. But I can't seem to help it. I don't know what to do.

Questions for Discussion

1. Do you think Joyce's father has a right to tell her she shouldn't see Reuben anymore?

2. How would you handle the situation if you were Joyce's father?

3. Why do you think Joyce still sees Reuben even though he stands her up?

4. Why do you think Reuben is so defensive when Joyce confronts him?

5. Do you know other girls who date boys who treat them badly?

6. How common is it for teenagers to sneak out on dates?

DEATH AND DYING

A Classmate with a Terminal Illness

The action takes place in a corner of the cafeteria at lunchtime. **Spencer, Randy, Lisa,** *and* **Natalie** *are finishing their meal.*

Randy: You know, Spence, I think you acted like a jerk in English class today.

Spencer: What?

Randy: Mr. Thompkins is a pretty good guy.

Spencer: What is this? Are you and Thompkins going steady, or something?

Randy: I like that class, OK? He's a good teacher. He's just trying to do his job.

Spencer: Look, man, it's none of your business.

Randy: It *is* my business. I don't like the disruptions.

Spencer: Talk about *my* being a jerk! (*He picks up his tray, turns quickly, and leaves.*)

Randy: What's his problem?

Lisa: I've been in classes with him too. You just have to over-look it.

Randy: He's a spoiled rich kid. He gets everything he wants and doesn't do anything. If I didn't know better, I'd think he was stupid. He never does his assignments.

Natalie: That's his choice, isn't it?

Randy: Yeah, but when Mr. Thompkins asked him to read something in class, he refused. Then he started mouthing off. Like I said, the guy's a jerk.

Lisa: Maybe he has a reason.

Randy: Like what?

Lisa: (*Sighs.*) Nobody's supposed to know this, Randy. But maybe it'll get you off his case.

Randy: (*Snapping at her.*) What's *that* supposed to mean?

Lisa: (*Looking at* **Natalie.**) You don't know either, do you?

Natalie: Know what? Something about Spence?

Lisa: That's right.

Natalie: I don't know anything about him. I know it's just like Randy said. He refuses to do any of his work. But he's OK. I mean, I like him all right.

Lisa: (*Looking back and forth between* **Natalie** *and* **Randy.**) If I tell you something, will you promise it won't go any further?

Randy shrugs and **Lisa** nods.

Lisa: (*Taking a deep breath.*) Spence has this disease. And when you have it, you don't live very long.

Randy: You're kidding! You've got to be kidding.

Lisa: I'm afraid not.

Natalie: How do you know? He looks OK. I mean, he looks perfectly healthy. He doesn't seems sick.

Lisa: When my mom was at the doctor's office, she overheard the doctor talking to Spence's mother.

Randy: I can't believe this. I've known the guy for years.

Lisa: He probably won't live through his twenties.

Randy: Oh, man. I called him a jerk.

Lisa: (*Trying to smile.*) Well, he is. Sometimes. But I guess he figures there's no point in school. If you know you're going to die in a few years, what's the use?

Natalie: I can't believe this. He seems so...happy, I suppose. Sure, he's irresponsible, but he's always friendly. He's always laughing.

Lisa: Yeah. I don't think I could be that way. I can't even put myself in his place. I hardly ever think about death, my own death. I know some time it will happen. But it's unreal. It's out there, somewhere, but it's like I have forever.

Randy: No wonder he's so spoiled. I guess I'd spoil my kids, too, if I knew they were going to die.

Natalie: (*Speaking to* **Lisa**.) He doesn't want anyone to know?

Lisa: I guess he thinks it will change the way people treat him.

Natalie: How'd your mom find out?

Lisa: I told you. She heard Dr. Brody talking to Spence's mother.

Randy: Wow. I don't know how you can handle something like that.

Lisa: Anyhow, Mom and Dad were talking about it. Then Mom found out Spence's family doesn't want anyone else to know. They want Spence to have as normal a life as possible.

Natalie: But now we do know. And what does that do? Every time I look at him, I'll think about it.

Randy: Man, I should apologize. But then he'll think something's up, won't he? I mean he'll start to wonder. (*He turns to* **Lisa**.) I'm glad you told me. It helps me to understand a little about why he acts like he does. But, in a way, I wish I didn't know. It... It changes everything.

Questions for Discussion

1. Why does Spencer act the way he does?

2. Is Spencer in a stage of denial or acceptance? What makes you think so?

3. Do you think Lisa should have told Randy and Natalie? How does it complicate things for them?

4. Discuss the pros and cons of family's "spoiling" the child who has an incurable illness.

5. How can Randy, Natalie, and Lisa help Spencer without telling him they know about his illness?

A Parent Dying

The action takes place at Jocelyn's home.
Keely *has previously called to tell* **Jocelyn** *she needs to
talk to someone.*

Jocelyn: (*Answering the door.*) Hi, Keely, come on in.

Keely: (*Crying as she enters.*) Oh, Joce.

Jocelyn: No one's home but me. We can talk. (*She leads the
way to the sofa, where the two girls sit.*) What is it, Keely?
What's wrong?

Keely: It's my mom. I can't believe it. (*She tries to stop crying.*)
Well, you know she went to the hospital.

Jocelyn: You told me. She was having back pains. Isn't that
what you said?

Keely: Daddy was waiting for me when I got home from school.
He was really upset. I've never seen him like that before.

Jocelyn: What did they find out, Keely?

Keely: She has...she has cancer. All through her. There's
nothing they can do. Chemotherapy, Dad said, and

maybe radiation treatments. But— (*She starts crying again.*) That will only delay things a little while.

Jocelyn: (*Putting her arm around Keely's shoulder.*) Oh, Keely.

Keely: I can't believe my mom's going to die. I mean, you always know that you'll probably live longer than your parents, but I never thought it would happen so soon.

Jocelyn: I know. I'm sure you don't want to hear this now. But when Daddy was sick, after we knew he was going to die, those were some of the happiest times.

Keely: I don't understand.

Jocelyn: In a way, you're lucky. You have some warning. I don't mean you can prepare for what's going to happen. You can't. Even though you know someone's going to die, it's a terrible shock when they do.

Keely: I didn't go to see her tonight. She's going to wonder why. I hate to do that to her. I'm being selfish. But I just can't face her yet.

Jocelyn: Does she know?

Keely: I'm not sure. I don't even know how to act around her. I'm afraid that I'll cry the whole time I'm at the hospital.

Jocelyn: What I started to say, Keel, is that...it's hard to understand. But if your mom does have some time left, it can be a happy time.

Keely: (*Pulling away.*) What are you saying, Joce? I don't know what you're talking about.

Jocelyn: It's like...it's hard to explain. But it's like the time is so precious. You want to make the most of it. And that's what you do. That's what Mom and Dad and I did.

Keely: But I feel...completely lost. I can't even think of life without her. It's like she was...is a buffer, maybe, between me and the world. You know what I mean?

Jocelyn: I know. And it's going to take a long, long time to feel any better.

Keely: It's so new to me. That Mom's going to die. But do you know what I thought of?

Jocelyn: What, Keel?

Keely: That people say time heals.

Jocelyn: It does.

Keely: But maybe I don't want it to. I want to remember Mom always. Oh, Joce, don't you see? Memories fade. My great-grandma, I loved her too. And she died when I was just a kid. And I felt such hurt. But the memory's faded. (*She sobs.*) I don't want to forget Mom like I'm forgetting my great-grandma.

Jocelyn: Your mother's so important to you. The good memories will remain. But look, Keely, you have time yet. You said that. You'll be able to spend time with her.

Keely: You know what? I had the thought that I don't want to see her anymore. I don't want to prolong this. I don't want to remember her sick and hurting. What kind of a person am I, Joce?

Jocelyn: I felt that way too, at first, I guess. And when Dad got really bad, I didn't go to see him. He was in the hospital—the last time—for three months. I went to see him only twice. What kind of a person does that make me?

Keely: You felt the same way?

Jocelyn: Yes, I guess I did. And for a long time I couldn't forgive myself. But when Mom would come home and talk about how bad Daddy was, I just couldn't take it. I tried to block it out. I didn't want to see him with tubes and oxygen and with his hair all gone. (Jocelyn's eyes fill with tears.) But I know now that it was natural to feel that way. I wasn't some kind of horrible person. (*She tries to smile.*) It took me a long time to forgive myself for that. And for other things, too.

Keely: What do you mean?

Jocelyn: For all the things I did to make Dad mad. For upsetting him. For all the trouble I caused him.

Keely: I know.

Jocelyn: Look, Keely, any time you need to talk, let me know, OK? Sometimes, it just helps to talk.

Questions for Discussion

1. Do you feel Jocelyn is a good listener? Why or why not?

2. Can you give an example of Jocelyn's using active listening?

3. According to Elizabeth Kubler-Ross, there are five stages a person goes through when confronted with death or dying. Investigate the stages and decide which one you think Keely is experiencing.

4. Discuss ways to deal with guilt feelings like Keely has when she does not go to the hospital to see her mother.

5. If Jocelyn were a peer counselor, what are some of the ways her conversation with Keely would be different?

Experiencing Guilt over a Death

Scene i

The action takes place in a hospital parking lot.

Ian: I can't believe this. I can't.

Candace: (*Crying.*) Bill was alive just an hour ago.

Ian: I can't live with this. It's my fault. It's all my fault. He didn't want to go with me. I talked him into it.

Candace: You shouldn't blame yourself.

Ian: That guy in the truck didn't even look. We had the right of way. He didn't even look.

Candace: It's like it's not real. Like the whole thing's a nightmare.

Ian: It's real all right. I wish it wasn't.

*A man enters and walks toward **Ian** and **Candace**. It's Bill's father, **Mr. Raymond**.*

Mr. Raymond: I knew you were out here. I had to come and see you. He's my son, and this is going to take a long time getting used to. It still hasn't sunk in. That he's gone.

Ian: Mr. Raymond, I don't know what to say. I'm really, really sorry.

Mr. Raymond: What... How did it happen?

Ian: (*Rubbing a hand across his eyes.*) I asked Bill to go for a bike ride. I just got my new ten-speed and wanted to try it out. (*His voice breaks.*) Bill didn't want to go. He said he had homework. But I kept insisting. And he gave in.

Mr. Raymond: (*Placing a hand on Ian's shoulder.*) It must have been awful. Seeing it happen.

Ian: We stopped at the intersection, and no one was coming. Suddenly, this pickup truck came out of nowhere. The driver didn't see us until it was too late. He tried to miss us, but... It happened so fast. Bill was beside me, and then he was lying in the street. He was dead. And I wasn't even hurt.

Mr. Raymond: (*Again squeezing Ian's shoulder.*) I've got to get back. My wife's still in the waiting room.

Ian: But you don't understand. It was all my fault. If I hadn't asked him to go... If I hadn't insisted...

Blackout.

Scene ii

The lights come up in a peer counseling class.

Ian: So, you see, it was my fault. And I can't live with the guilt. I should be dead, not Bill.

Carrie: I know it must seem that way, Ian. But you didn't know it would happen.

Ian: But he didn't want to go. He finally gave in, just because we were friends. I'm going to have to live with that forever.

Carrie: Ian?

Ian: Yeah?

Carrie: From the way you described it, Bill's parents don't blame you. At least, his father doesn't blame you.

Ian: He doesn't. I don't know about his mother. She doesn't want to see me. She doesn't want to talk to me.

Melvin: Have you tried to talk to her?

Ian: At first I did. But not for a while.

Faye: Then you don't really know that she blames you.

Ian: I guess not.

Faye: Maybe she couldn't face anyone. Bill was her only son. Maybe it was her way of grieving.

Ian: (*Shrugs.*) I don't know. It doesn't matter, does it? Whether or not she blames me.

Carrie: It seems to matter to you.

Ian: You know, every day when I wake up, I look out the window and see the sun. And I wonder why I'm still alive when Bill is dead?

Faye: You aren't thinking of...suicide, are you?

Ian: What's the difference if I live or die?

Carrie: You have everything to live for. A whole lifetime.

Ian: Why?

Carrie: You're really feeling this, Ian. Have you talked to anyone?

Ian: A shrink? No.

Melvin: Do you think maybe you should? A lot of people care about you, Ian. Really. Just think about it. Your family, your friends. Even...even Mr. Raymond, right? He wouldn't have come out there that night to talk to you if he didn't. Now isn't that true?

Ian: (*Frowning.*) I... I suppose.

Melvin: Then, obviously, it would only make matters worse, wouldn't it? If you weren't around anymore.

Ian: I caused someone else to die. Someone I cared about. I loved him more than a brother.

Faye: What's it been? At least three months? Don't you think —

Ian: I know you're all trying to help. But he was my best friend. Don't you understand?

Questions for Discussion

1. Ian feels a great sense of guilt over Bill's death. Discuss ways to deal with guilt feelings.

2. Why do you think Mrs. Raymond doesn't want to see Ian?

3. What should the members of the peer counseling class do when they suspect Ian might be suicidal?

4. Discuss forgiveness. What are the steps that need to be taken when a person needs to forgive himself or herself?

DECISION MAKING

The Crime of Stealing

The action takes place behind the counter of a small restaurant just after closing time. **Emmet** *and* **Tabitha** *are cleaning up.*

Emmet: Boy, I don't know.

Tabitha: What don't you know?

Emmet: I'm not a snitch, but that new guy...

Tabitha: You noticed too, huh?

Emmet: How can I help it? It's like he doesn't care who sees what he does.

Judy: (*Coming out of the back room.*) About ready to go?

Tabitha: We were just talking about that new guy, Roy. Are you aware of what he's doing?

Judy: I try not to be.

Emmet: But you see what he does.

Judy: It's no concern of mine.

Tabitha: One of these days, Mr. Ernst is going to figure out what's going on.

Emmet: Not "one of these days," Tab. He's no dummy.

Judy: Live and let live, OK?

Tabitha: I don't like what's going on. Roy has to be sticking ten or fifteen dollars in his pocket every day. And I know he's cheating the customers. Overcharging and not ringing it up.

Judy: That's his business.

Emmet: I'm not going to take the rap for something I didn't do. Besides that, I don't like the guy.

Judy: Well, it just so happens, I do.

Emmet: Fine, you just go on liking him all you want. But something's got to be done.

Tabitha: Do you think we should tell Mr. Ernst?

Emmet: I don't know. Like I said, I'm not a snitch. On the other hand...

Judy: You know he can't fire us. Not without proof.

Emmet: What do you mean?

Judy: Just what I said. If he fires us without cause, he's going to have a lawsuit staring him right in the face.

Emmet: You mean Ernst has go to catch Roy red-handed or it's no-go?

Judy: You bet your bottom dollar. And that's hard to do. In fact, I'm going to make it even harder. I'm going to tell Roy what's going on. With you two, I mean.

Emmet: Why? What good's that going to do?

Judy: I like Roy. I told you that.

Tabitha: What you seem to be saying, Judy, is that you condone Roy's stealing. Is that it?

Judy: No, it isn't. What I'm saying is that I'm not going to interfere where it's not my business.

Tabitha: But you will interfere if you tell Roy that we've seen what he's been doing.

Judy: If you talk to Ernst, it'll just be your word against mine.

Emmet: What do you mean?

Judy: If you try to get Roy fired, I'll tell Ernst you're protecting yourself.

Tabitha: What if there are two of us?

Judy: Big deal. I don't think you'll risk that. Anyway, what's Mr. Ernst to you?

Tabitha: First of all, he's a nice man. He's more than fair. Starting wage here's higher than anywhere else around. We get raises more often.

Judy: So?

Emmet: What does that mean?

Judy: Why should I feel any loyalty for him? He's well off. He lives high on the hog.

Tabitha: What you're saying is that it's OK to steal from someone if you just happen to think he can afford to lose the money.

Judy: Something like that.

Tabitha: Well, I think you're wrong. Dead wrong.

Judy: We'll just have to see about that, won't we?

Questions for Discussion

1. Discuss your perception of employee-employer relations when stealing is involved.

2. Judy says, "It's no concern of mine." What are the pros and cons of doing this?

3. Discuss Tabitha's and Emmet's options.

4. If Tabitha and Emmet decide to talk to Mr. Ernst, what approach do you think they should use?

5. Discuss the future working relationship among Tabitha, Emmet, and Judy. List positive ways they can work together.

6. Discuss Judy's attraction to Roy in relationship to her job.

Sexual Blackmail

The action occurs in a peer counseling class.

Neala: I don't know what to do.

Megan: What is it, Neala?

Neala: Well, some of you know my boyfriend. His name is Chuck.

Several of the students nod.

Neala: I hate to have you think I'm bad-mouthing him for no real reason. (*She glances into the faces of those around her.*) I guess there's nothing to do but say it. He's trying to blackmail me.

Austin: Wow! I've known Chuck since kindergarten. That's hard to believe.

Neala: I know you're friends. That's one reason why it's so hard to talk about this. But I don't know what to do.

Burt: What's he doing, Neala? I mean, trying to get money from you or something?

Neala: (*Laughs bitterly.*) I wish it were that simple, but it isn't.

Megan: Like Austin said, we're here to listen, if you want us to.

Neala: It... It has to do with sex.

Megan: Is Chuck trying to force you to do something you don't believe in?

Neala: (*Grateful for Megan's perception of the situation.*) Yes.

Austin: If you don't want to do what he asks, can't you just refuse?

Neala: (*In a small voice.*) He knows something, Austin. Something I did once. He said he'd tell my parents about it if I don't... (*Her voice breaks.*) If I don't...

Burt: What you did, Neala. Is it really that bad?

Neala *nods.*

Burt: Something you're ashamed of? That you don't want people to know?

Neala: He's going to tell my parents. They want me to go to college. To one of the top schools, and there's so much pressure. I mean I have to be way up there to be considered. And even then, there's no guarantee.

Austin: What is it that he's holding over you?

Neala: I cheated. I cheated on this exam. I've never done that before. I did it only that one time. I stole a copy of the answer sheet. It bothered me so much I told Chuck what I'd done. I showed him the answer sheet, and he wouldn't give it back.

Megan: I can see why you're scared.

Austin: I can't believe Chuck would do that.

Neala: Me, neither. I couldn't believe it. And maybe he wouldn't. Things just got... They got so heavy with him one time. He didn't want to stop. We were in his car, parked in this...this lane outside of town. What am I going to do?

Burt: What do you think is the worst thing that could happen?

Neala: My parents! I don't even care about college. (*She shakes her head.*) No, that's not true. I really do. But if he tells my parents, they'd be so disappointed.

Burt: That time in the car, was it the only time he threatened to tell?

Neala: It was the first time.

Austin: You mean this kept up?

Neala: I don't even know if he was serious. Afterwards, I mean. That first time, yeah. But when he'd bring it up later, it was like he was kidding. Some big joke, huh?

Austin: Did you try to talk to him about it?

Neala: No, no, I didn't. (*Speaking to* **Austin**.) You said you've known him since kindergarten.

Austin nods.

Neala: I've known him a long time too. But lately, I don't think I know him at all.

Questions for Discussion

1. How do you feel about Neala's cheating?

2. How do you feel about Chuck's trying to blackmail her?

3. Do you think Chuck is kidding about telling? Is he just applying a little peer pressure?

4. What could Neala have done differently?

5. Is Neala really worried about how her parents would react?

Teens Who Envy

The action takes place in the school cafeteria at lunchtime. **Faith** *and* **Lori** *are sitting across from each other at a long table. At the far end is* **Brad**. *Finishing his lunch,* **Brad** *picks up his tray and walks past the girls.*

Brad: Hi, Faith. Lori. How you doing?

Faith: Hi, Brad. That was a quick lunch.

Brad: Growing boys like me work up an appetite.

Faith *laughs, but* **Lori** *is not amused.*

Lori: (*Mocking.*) "Growing boys like me." (*In a normal tone.*) Who does he think he is, anyhow?

Faith: Brad?

Lori: Yeah, Brad. He's nothing but a spoiled brat.

Faith: (*Surprised.*) I gather you don't like him.

Lori: The boy who has everything? I'm afraid not.

106

Faith: So he's rich, so what?

Lori: Why are you defending him all of a sudden?

Faith: What's wrong with him? I like him. Maybe you just don't know him.

Lori: What's to know?

Faith: Like I said, he's a good kid.

Lori: He can afford to be. He can afford anything he wants.

Faith: I get it. Just because he has a rich dad, that makes him a jerk.

Lori: That isn't what I said.

Faith: I think you're jealous.

Lori: So what if I am?

Faith: Look, Lori, Brad can't help who his parents are.

Lori: What is this? Is he your boyfriend?

Faith: You know better than that.

Lori: You mean, why would a boy from the rich part of town go for a girl like you?

Faith: No, that isn't what I mean. I mean that he's just a friend.

Lori: You call him a friend. He's nothing but an egotistical—

Faith: He is not.

Lori: (*Surprised.*) Why are you sticking up for him so much?

Faith: Why are you attacking him?

Lori: I don't have to listen to this. I thought we were friends. I thought we cared about each other. And you choose that...that stuck-up goon over me.

> **Lori** *jumps up, grabs her tray and stalks off. For a moment* **Faith** *sits by herself, randomly jabbing a fork into what's left of her lunch. She doesn't see* **Brad** *coming back.*

Brad: Mind if I sit down?

Faith: I thought you'd gone.

Brad: Just cleaning off my tray. (*Sitting beside her.*) I couldn't help but hear what was going on. I mean, I wasn't trying to eavesdrop, but Lori's voice *does* carry. (*Pause.*) It's kind of dumb, but anyhow, thanks.

Faith: Lori can't help it, I guess. It's just the way she is. But you can't help it either.

Brad: I suppose everyone is envious of someone. Or something.

Faith: Maybe. But most of the time, it's just a passing thought. Except maybe for young kids.

Brad: (*Smiling.*) You know who I envy?

Faith: Who?

Brad: You, and, well, Lori too.

Faith: For heaven's sake, why?

Brad: I've never talked about this to anyone before. But sometimes I wish I could escape. Sure, I like to be able to get pretty much what I want, but...

Faith: But what?

Brad: This is really weird. I have this darned...responsibility, I guess. This thing where, somehow, I have to be perfect, you know?

Faith: What do you mean?

Brad: There are lots of people like Lori. I mean, in the respect that they're envious.

Faith: Jealous, you mean.

Brad: OK then, jealous. Anyhow, I feel as if they're judging me all the time. There's this gigantic spotlight following me everywhere I go. (*Laughs.*) Not really, but because of my background, my family, everything I do is judged. Is looked at. I hate it. Once in a while, I just want to be me. I just want to be like everyone else.

Faith: Wow. I never would have thought of that.

Brad: Sure, having parents who are well off is pretty darned nice, most of the time. I'm the first to admit it. But at other times...I'd just like to be one of the crowd. You know?

Questions for Discussion

1. Are Lori's actions typical?

2. Whose behavior is more typical, Lori's or Faith's?

3. Do you admire Brad? Why or why not? Do you believe him when he says he would like to be one of the crowd?

4. Why does Brad say he envies Faith and Lori?

5. Is Brad exaggerating his feelings of responsibility?

6. Do you think people make a conscious decision to act certain ways toward their peers? Why or why not?

Uncontrolled Temper

The action takes place in the high school courtyard.
Sid, Charlie, Shelly *and* **Yvonne** *are seated around a small table.*

Sid: You know, Paige would be a nice girl if she didn't fly off the handle so much. I mean, we have a lot in common, and I enjoy being with her.

Shelly: Have you told her how you feel?

Sid: Yeah, last night, and that made her even angrier. She called me names, slammed the car door, and took off toward her house. It was a couple of miles.

Charlie: You didn't let her walk home, did you?

Sid: I caught up with her and tried to talk her into getting back inside the car. She wouldn't pay any attention. Then this old guy pops up out of nowhere and tells me "the young lady wants to be left alone."

Yvonne: My grandma always uses the expression about cutting off your nose to spite your face. Well, that's a good description of Paige. It's like she's never in control. If I were you, I'd forget her.

Shelly: Hey, is this Paige we're talking about? I mean we've all been friends for years. You just can't write her off like that.

Yvonne: Even when she acts like a jerk? It's like she's a spoiled brat. If things don't go her way, she throws a tantrum.

Sid: I think you're wrong, Yvonne. I don't think it's because she's spoiled. She's had a pretty rough life.

Yvonne: OK, I agree. But who can put up with it? I mean, it's OK to be understanding and all that. But there comes a time when people have to be responsible for their own lives.

Charlie: Sure, they do, ideally. But you know darn well that's rough. Everyone — and I mean everyone — has hangups and problems. They wouldn't be human if they didn't.

Shelly: I used to try. I really did. But I could only be yelled at so many times. And, hey, I react to that. We all know Paige has good points. She's generous — with her time as well as her possessions. She has a great sense of humor. She's fun to be around. Except...

Sid: Like you said, Shelly, we've all been friends for a long time. But unless you're blind, you know it's gone much beyond that with me. I mean, I care about her. I know we're young, but I've thought of spending the rest of my life with her. And you know what? That's a good thought. It makes me feel great, except for that temper. I can't deal with it.

Yvonne: Like last week, Paige and I went shopping. She was buying a knit top. We were at this big department store, and the cashier asked us to move to the other side of the desk because the register we went to was closed. That's all she asked. That we move to the other side. And Paige lost it. She screamed at the poor girl, slammed down the top, and tore out of the store. Now that's not your everyday kind of behavior.

Charlie: I've often thought that maybe her flying off the handle does indicate a deeper problem, one she doesn't want to discuss. Maybe she won't even face it herself.

Shelly: But until she does, don't you think it's her problem? I mean nobody can force her to face herself.

Sid: You know, I think we're getting way off base here. We're not a bunch of shrinks.

The others laugh. **Paige** *enters
and crosses to sit beside* **Sid.**

Paige: Hi, everyone.

There is a moment of strained silence.

Sid: How are you doing, Paige?

Paige: (*Not looking at him.*) Great. How about you?

Sid: Paige, about last night.

Paige: (*Turning to* **Sid** *and smiling brightly.*) What about last night? I had a great time, didn't you? It was a wonderful film.

Sid: I mean...about afterwards.

Paige: I don't know what you mean.

Sid: Look, Paige —

Paige: No, you look, Sid. It's a beautiful day. I'm in a great mood, and I don't want it ruined.

One by one, **Charlie, Shelly,** *and* **Yvonne** *stand up and leave the table.*

Sid: OK, Paige. (*He starts to rise, but her words force him back down.*)

Paige: Why did you have to bring up what happened? Look at the result. Everyone left. You've driven them all away.

Questions for Discussion

1. Discuss Paige's behavior. Why do you think she acts the way she does?

2. Do you agree or disagree with Yvonne's advice, "If I were you, I'd forget her"?

3. Discuss Sid's loyalty to Paige. Name some characteristics of loyalty.

4. Do you think Sid should have brought up the previous night's problem? Why or why not?

5. Sid said he might want to spend the rest of his life with Paige. Would you marry someone with a bad temper? Why or why not?

A Matter of Priorities

The action occurs in a music studio. **Melissa** *is sitting at a piano as her teacher walks back and forth in front of a window.*

Teacher: I don't understand what's happening. You've always been my star pupil. For years, you've practiced like you were supposed to. Now, all of a sudden, you seem to have lost interest.

Melissa: I haven't lost interest. I'm just tired. I've been practicing since I was five. I'm seventeen now. I need a year off.

Teacher: You start college next year. Now's the time you should be working your hardest. You want to be accepted into a good music school, don't you? Maybe even earn a scholarship.

Melissa: Of course, I do. But...

Teacher: But what?

Melissa: But I want other things, too.

Teacher: Such as?

Melissa: I want to enjoy my last year of high school.

Teacher: What does that have to do with your playing? Haven't you enjoyed school so far and still found time to practice?

Melissa: I've never had time for extra-curricular activities. I always had to go home and practice.

Teacher: You've had time for friends.

Melissa: Not really. I don't have any close friends. I'm never available to do things with them. On weekends, I'm usually in a workshop or playing in some competition. I turned my friends down so many times, they stopped asking.

Teacher: But it's paid off. Look at your awards, all the recognition you've received. Your parents are proud. I'm proud.

Melissa: That's just the point. I've done what I was supposed to do. What everyone *else* wanted. Now I want some time off — to do what I want to do.

Teacher: (*Growing impatient.*) And just what is it you want to do?

Melissa: I want to go to football games without worrying about getting home to be rested for the next day's competition. I want to play tennis in the afternoons. I want to have time to meet boys and go on dates.

Teacher: Have you talked this over with your parents?

Melissa: No, I wanted to talk to you first. I thought you might help me tell them that I need a break before I go to college.

Teacher: You don't need a break from your lessons or practice. You worked too hard all these years to throw it away.

Melissa: I'm not throwing it away. I just want to put it on hold. I'll start practicing as soon as graduation is over. I'll practice all summer. I'll be in good shape for college.

Teacher: Melissa, didn't you hear what I said earlier about getting accepted? How can you audition for music departments if you don't practice? And think of the money you could save your parents if you won a scholarship.

Melissa: But what about what *I* want?

Teacher: Look at your parents' sacrifices so you could have lessons and attend the best workshops to study with master teachers. It would break your parents' hearts if you gave that all up now.

Melissa: Look, Mrs. Shaffer, I appreciate what my parents have done, and I don't plan to give it up.

Teacher: (*Deliberately misunderstanding.*) Good. I'm glad to hear you say that. You had me concerned for a moment.

Melissa: I'll always have my music. It's a part of my life. I'm not just going to throw it away. But I want one year off. Then I'll be ready to work hard. I heard Cindy say that she has to practice five or six hours every day in college. I want a break before I bury myself in a practice hall.

Teacher: Well, we can talk again next week. Let's not waste any more of your lesson time today. (*Sitting in a chair by the piano.*) I want you to play the Chopin concerto. I know you've made progress on it.

Melissa *sighs and opens her music book.*

Questions for Discussion

1. List the pros and cons of Melissa's taking a year off from her music.

2. Do you feel Melissa should be the person to make that decision, or should it be her parents? Why?

3. What part, if any, should the music teacher play in making the decision?

4. What are some pros and cons of being dedicated to a talent or a sport?

5. What other options do you think Melissa has?

DEPRESSION

Unable to Live Up to Expectations

The action takes place in a peer counseling setting.

Nolan: I'm really depressed, and I don't know what to do about it.

Winona: Any particular reason for feeling that way?

Nolan: Yeah, I guess, but it's kind of dumb.

Drew: Do you want to tell us about it?

Nolan: It's the speech team.

Winona: What do you mean?

Nolan: Well, you know, we have this forensics team. We compete in a lot of tournaments. Debate, extemporaneous, monologues, that kind of thing.

Winona: You're on the team.

Nolan: In extemporaneous.

Drew: What does that mean, exactly?

Nolan: Well, everyone draws a topic and then has a little while to prepare a speech about it. We're judged on how well we do.

Winona: Wow, if I had to compete in something like that, I'd be depressed too.

Nolan: That's not it. I like it. I enjoy doing that kind of thing. Or, at least, I did.

Jane: You did? You don't anymore?

Nolan: That's the whole problem, and, like I said, it's really dumb. (*Sighs.*) I didn't make State this year.

Jane: The State Tournament, you mean.

Nolan: Yeah.

Drew: Why is that so bad?

Nolan: It's like I have to be the best at everything, or I'm not good at anything.

Winona: I don't understand.

Nolan: If I'm not the best, then I've failed.

Jane: Nobody can be the best at everything.

Nolan: I know that. In my head, I know that.

Winona: But it doesn't help, huh?

Nolan: The last two years I went to State, I placed third sophomore year and won last year. This year, nothing. I came in sixth in the district, so I couldn't go on to State competition. And it was like, wow, I'd really let everyone down.

Jane: How do you mean that?

Nolan: My parents, the school, myself.

Drew: It's funny, but you just mentioned your parents first. Then the school, then yourself.

Nolan: If I'm not the best, if I don't come in first, then I'm nothing. To my parents I'm nothing, and to me, too.

Winona: Are you sure your parents really feel that way?

Nolan: No, I'm not sure. (*Shakes his head.*) But they're the perfect couple. They're good at everything. My mom was valedictorian of her class. My dad was first-string quarterback for three years in high school. How can I compete with them?

Jane: Why do you have to try? You're you. You're not your parents.

Nolan: But I've got to. Otherwise, I'm a big disappointment to them.

Drew: How do you know that?

Nolan: I can tell.

Drew: What do you mean?

Nolan *shrugs.*

Drew: Nolan, you have to be your own person, you know? The only one you have to please is yourself.

Nolan: I hear what you're saying, Drew. Maybe you're right. And Winona, too. But still, I have these feelings. And, you know, sometimes I just don't think life is worth it.

Questions for Discussion

1. Does Nolan say anything that makes you think his depression is serious?

2. What is your thought when Nolan says, "Sometimes I just don't think life is worth it"?

3. Do you think Nolan wants to be perfect to please his parents or himself?

4. Do you think Nolan did his best when he came in sixth?

5. What could be some reasons for his low placement at the district level, after going to state level two years in a row?

Dealing with Depression

*The action occurs as **Betsy** and **Katie** sit on a bench
on a high school campus.*

Betsy: My mom keeps asking me why. My teachers want to know what's wrong. My friends are getting fed up because I can't give them any reasons.

Katie: Are you saying that you really don't know?

Betsy: I'm saying there's no reason. No reason at all.

Katie: It must be frustrating to be depressed and not know why.

Betsy: If I could figure out why, maybe I could do something about it.

Katie: Did anything happen to get this all started?

Betsy: No. If I'd had a fight with my parents or blown a test, then I'd understand. I thought if I talked to you, you might be able to help. Since you're a peer counselor, you might have seen others with my problem.

Katie: No two problems are ever alike. But I have listened when kids talked about being depressed. Usually they know why, and they just need to deal with it.

Betsy: I've read most of the library books on depression, and I know the ways you're supposed to deal with it. But nothing works for me.

Katie: How long has this been going on?

Betsy: About six months. Some days are much worse than others.

Katie: What do you mean?

Betsy: I started out just being a little down. Then I got worse and worse. Some days, I just want to stay in bed. I want to pull the covers over my head and not have to deal with anything.

Katie: Do you think you need to see a professional? Someone trained to treat depression?

Betsy: A psychiatrist, you mean?

Katie: Someone like that.

Betsy: My parents don't believe in doctors.

Katie: Have you talked to your parents about how you're feeling?

Betsy: Yes. I was scared. I told them I thought that something was really wrong.

Katie: What did they say?

Betsy: That it's a stage I'm going through. That I'll get over it.

Katie: How do you feel about that?

Betsy: It's not just a stage. If I had problems, sure, I could understand. But I don't.

Katie: I know you get good grades.

Betsy: I'm lucky I guess. Schoolwork has always come easy.

Katie: How nice that must be.

Betsy: It certainly helps with college. Getting accepted, I mean. Actually, I can go to any college I want. My grandma left me money for that in her will.

Katie: Like you said, you're lucky.

Betsy: In many ways, I am. I have a good home, lots of friends. What more could I possibly want? That's why I don't understand the depression, why I think something's really wrong.

Katie: Like what?

Betsy: A brain tumor, maybe. I don't know. I lie awake at night wondering what's going to happen next.

Katie: How would your parents feel about your seeing someone who's not an M.D.?

Betsy: A psychologist or something? I don't know. No one in our family has gone to anyone like that before. But I'm scared. I'm really getting scared.

Katie: I want to help you, but I'm not trained to handle serious problems like depression. Peer counselors aren't mini- psychologists, and we certainly don't pretend to be. If you had a fight with your boyfriend or something and needed to talk out the hurt and anger, I'd listen. But your case is different.

Betsy: I know. I've been depressed in the past over things like having a friend move away. But that feeling wasn't like this one. It hangs on, day after day. That's what scares me. Particularly since I can't come up with any reason for it.

Katie: Would you like me to talk to your mom and dad about the possibility of your seeing a psychologist or a mental health counselor?

Betsy: No, you can't do that — at least not till I check it out and see if they approve.

Katie: Would you find out before we talk next time? I also want to talk to my peer counseling teacher and see what she suggests.

Betsy: Anything you can do to help, I'll appreciate.

Questions for Discussion

1. Describe some of the symptoms of depression.

2. When should a peer counselor refer a counselee to a professional?

3. What other alternatives does Betsy have if her parents will not allow her to see a mental health professional?

4. Discuss Katie's role as a peer counselor. Is there anything you would have done differently if you'd been the peer counselor?

DIVORCE

Choosing Between Parents

The action takes place in the living room of Pam Snyder's house. **Pam** *is talking with her best friend,* **Sibyl**. *Both girls are seated on the sofa.*

Pam: (*In tears.*) They're totally tearing me apart. I mean, I love both of them, but they can't seem to accept that.

Sibyl: I don't understand.

Pam: They hate each other, I guess. And that's hard enough by itself. But because of that, they both think I should take sides.

Sibyl: They actually said that?

Pam: Not in so many words. But it's like if Mom says something about Dad, she thinks I should agree. And Dad's the same way.

Sibyl: So what are you going to do?

Pam: I don't know. But it's gotten so bad that my stomach hurts all the time, and I can't sleep and I can't concentrate on anything. My grades are terrible. I know I should care about that, but I can't, not now.

Sibyl: Your mom and dad aren't still together, are they?

Pam: No way! Maybe that's one thing I should be thankful for. At least they're not fighting all the time.

Sibyl: But in some ways, it's worse.

Pam: Yeah. Because I'm supposed to choose. I mean, when they fought before, they didn't try to drag me into it. Oh, sometimes, Mom would try to talk to me about how bad Dad is, and he'd tell me about all of Mom's supposed faults. But not very often.

Sibyl: Maybe things will settle down when the divorce is final. It isn't final yet, is it?

Pam: (*Very quietly.*) No. And I'm dreading when it is.

Sibyl: You mean there's hope they'll get back together?

Pam: (*Sighs.*) No. I'm sure that's impossible.

Sibyl: Then maybe that for the best.

Pam: No! (*Shaking her head.*) You don't understand. I'm going to have to make a choice.

Sibyl: What kind of choice?

Pam: You're lucky, Sibyl. Your mom and dad get along. They really seem to like each other, to respect each other. I never really thought about that until...

Sibyl: I guess I am lucky. Funny, isn't it? You never really think about your parents. I mean, you never think about their relationship. They're just kind of there.

Pam: I know. But then something happens, and your whole world falls apart.

Sibyl: It's that bad, huh?

Pam: Maybe I'm being a baby.

Sibyl: Of course, you're not. I'm glad you feel we can talk about it.

Pam: (*Trying to smile.*) Thanks. (*Pause.*) I have to choose between them. Who I want to live with, I mean.

Sibyl: Won't the judge just award custody?

Pam: No. That would be easier. But since I'm as old as I am, it's up to me.

Sibyl: That's terrible.

Pam: I know. But I have to decide. And I love them both. Oh, I do truly love them both. And I know one of them's going to be hurt. Still, it's up to me to decide which one I'm going to live with.

Sibyl: I'd hate to be in your shoes. (*Pause.*) Maybe if you tried to make a list.

Pam: A list? What are you talking about?

Sibyl: Pros and cons.

Pam: Of my parents? I can't do that. I couldn't do that. I told you, I love both of them.

Sibyl: I don't mean that.

Pam: What do you mean?

Sibyl: Things like, where are they going to live? Would you have to change schools to live with either one of them? I suppose your mom's going to keep the house?

Pam: I don't know. Sometimes she says she wants to. Then she says she wants a clean break with the past. She doesn't want anything to remind her...

Sibyl: Will your dad keep it then?

Pam: Who knows?

Sibyl: Look, Pam, I think maybe you should try to find out. So you can make the best choice.

Pam: The best choice? Sibyl, haven't you heard what I've been saying?

Sibyl: (*Squeezing Pam's hand.*) I know, Pam. It's hard. All I'm saying is that the more you know about the situation, the better. And just because you're living with one parent doesn't mean you're rejecting the other.

Pam: I guess not.

Sibyl: Of course it doesn't. The fact is there is only one Pam Snyder. You can't be two places at once. But you can be two places at different times.

Pam: I don't understand.

Sibyl: Weekends, summer vacation. Can't you spend those times with the parent you don't live with?

Pam: I suppose.

Sibyl: You'll work it out. I know you.

Pam: I hope so.

Questions for Discussion

1. What consequence of the divorce troubles Pam the most?

2. How do you feel about Sybil's suggestion that Pam make a list?

3. How do you think most teenagers feel about Sybil's statement, "You never really think about your parents. They're just kind of there"?

4. Who suffers more from a divorce — the parents or the children?

5. Should Sybil have said, "You'll work it out. I know you"? Why are "pat answers" usually avoided in good communication?

Wanting Parents to Divorce

The action occurs in a peer counseling class.

Tammy: I can't stand it any longer. I've got to get away for a few days.

Arnold: The same problems at home?

Tammy: Yes, but worse. Mom and Dad fight constantly. It used to be just weekends, but now it starts as soon as he walks in the door and keeps up for hours. When I go to bed, I put the pillow over my ears so I can't hear. By the time I get up, they're at it again.

Arnold: Sounds like a real battleground.

Tammy: At least soldiers rest between battles. At my house, there's no rest from it. It's awful. Just awful.

Lucy: My dad and mom used to fight, but they finally worked out the problem. Maybe the same thing will happen with your folks.

Tammy: I wish that could be true, but I don't think so. They fight about everything. It's getting to be too much for me. My grades are terrible.

Arnold: Have you talked to your parents about how its affecting you?

Tammy: I tried, but they treat me like a child. They tell me not to get involved. That it doesn't concern me or my sister. But it does. Julie cries herself to sleep almost every night. She's only six. She shouldn't have to deal with this kind of thing.

Arnold: You sound worried about her.

Tammy: I am. Things are so different now than a year ago. Mom used to read her stories every night and spend time with her. Now she hardly notices her.

Arnold: Do you think there's a chance things will improve?

Tammy: Not till they get a divorce.

Lucy: Would you like them to, do you think?

Tammy: Anything would be an improvement. Yes, I'd like them to. The sooner the better.

Arnold: What you're saying is serious stuff. My dad and mom are divorced, and it's no picnic for me or my brothers.

Tammy: I know. And I'd probably be sorry if one of them moved out. (*Sighs.*) I love them both. But right now, I think some peace and quiet would be wonderful.

Amy: I don't think parents realize how much their actions affect their kids. I know mine don't. They seem to think I don't know what's going on.

Tammy: Sounds like you have a problem too.

Amy: I just know Dad isn't away on business trips so much like Mom says he is.

Tammy: At least it's quiet at your house.

Amy: Would you like to stay over a few days?

Tammy: I wasn't hinting.

Amy: I know. I just think it would be nice to have you there for the weekend. You'd get away from your own situation, and it would keep me from getting bored.

Tammy: It sounds wonderful, but I'll have to check with Mom.

Arnold: Getting away would be nice, but it seems you need a more permanent solution to the problem. Is there anything you can do to help your parents settle their differences?

Amy: I think we all have to realize we're not responsible for making our parents' marriages work. We don't need to feel guilty when they don't.

Tammy: Right. Like I said, I'd be relieved if Mom and Dad got divorced. I'd feel the battle was over and certainly wouldn't feel guilty.

Questions for Discussion

1. Why does Tammy want her parents to get a divorce? Do you think there are other reasons besides those she states? Why or why not?

2. What responsibilities do you feel parents have in making the home a happy place for their children?

3. Amy says that children aren't responsible for making their parents' marriages work and shouldn't feel guilty if it isn't successful. Do you agree or disagree? Why?

4. Arnold cautions Tammy about wanting her parents to get a divorce. He says it's no picnic for him or his brothers. Discuss the effects of divorce on children in the home.

5. How can Tammy let her parents know the ways in which their actions are affecting her life?

A Divorced Father

The action takes place in a group setting.

Justin: I don't know what to do about my dad.

Alex: What's the matter, Justin?

Justin: He hasn't been himself since Mom left. I thought he'd just have to get used to the idea, but I was wrong. Things have gotten worse.

Betsy: Would you like to tell us about it?

Justin: It started about two years ago, when Dad got a promotion. He'd always worked long hours, but now he had to work even more. He was hardly ever home, not even on weekends.

Betsy: That must have been hard on the family.

Justin: Particularly Mom. My brothers and I had school, but she was home by herself. I guess she got pretty lonely.

Betsy: How did your father feel about it?

Justin: All he thought about was his job.

139

Betsy: I'm afraid that's true of a lot of men.

Justin: Not with Dad anymore — now that it's too late.

Alex: Because your mother moved out.

Justin: Yes. She met another guy, Steve, at some seminar. They started seeing each other on a regular basis.

Betsy: And your father didn't suspect anything?

Justin: Like I said, he was hardly ever home. And when he was home, he was too tired to notice much of anything.

Alex: So her moving out came as a shock?

Justin: They'd been married for twenty years.

Betsy: She must have been really lonely.

Justin: She was. Her own mom had just died, and that was bad enough. Then to have Dad away all the time...

Betsy: Then she met Steve.

Justin: Right.

Betsy: And he was just what she needed.

Justin: He's a nice person. Since the divorce, I've gotten to know him really well.

Betsy: So what happened to your dad when your mom moved out?

Justin: He fell apart. I wanted to stay with him so I wouldn't have to change schools. I was glad I did when I saw how much he needed me.

Betsy: It helps him to have you there?

Justin: I hope so. What's ironic is that he's been coming home at dinnertime, now that Mom's no longer there.

Alex: You said things have gotten worse.

Justin: He's like someone I don't even know. When Mom and Steve announced their engagement, Dad took it real hard.

Alex: There's no chance your mom and dad will get back together?

Justin: She definitely plans to marry Steve. The funny thing is, I can't blame her. I've never seen her so happy.

Betsy: But your dad's not happy.

Justin: He feels completely rejected.

Alex: Most men would, I think.

Justin: But he's being destructive.

Betsy: I don't follow.

Justin: You should see the women he's dating. His self-esteem must be awfully low.

Betsy: And you're worried about him?

Justin: With the kind of women he's been dating, anything can happen.

Betsy: I thought parents were supposed to stay up and worry about their kids, not the other way around.

Justin: It's almost like I'm the parent and he's the child.

Betsy: And you want the roles reversed again?

Justin: Yes, but I don't know how to do it. Any ideas?

Questions for Discussion

1. Discuss role reversals between a parent and a teenager.

2. What changes occurred in Justin's mother's life before she moved out of the house?

3. What do you think is making Justin's father react the way he is?

4. How can Justin get the roles reversed again?

5. Poor communication causes problems in many families. List the problems it's causing in Justin's family.

DRUGS

Drinking and Driving

The action occurs in a car. **Jeff** *is the driver.* **Linda** *sits beside him. In the back seat are* **Bob** *and* **Sue**. **Jeff** *is holding a bottle half-full of cheap wine.*

Jeff: (*Handing the bottle to* **Bob**.) Here, Bob, before Linda and I swig it all down. (*He laughs.*) Make sure Sue has some too.

Bob: (*Taking a swig and handing the bottle to* **Sue**.) Here you go.

Sue: (*Matter of factly.*) I don't drink.

Bob: You don't have to *drink*. Just take a sip. Join the party.

> **Sue** *shakes her head.* **Bob** *passes the bottle to* **Linda**, *who takes a drink.*

Jeff: (*Glancing at* **Linda**.) 'Atta-girl. You know how to have a good time. Maybe you should teach your cousin how to have some fun.

> **Linda** *laughs and passes the bottle to* **Jeff**.

144

Jeff: (*Joking.*) OK. Who drank more than his share? There's hardly any left. (*He chug-a-lugs till the bottle's empty.*)

Linda: (*Tugging playfully at Jeff's arm.*) Aren't you going to come up for air?

Bob: That's it. Now we're going to need more booze. There's a store up ahead, the next block. Pull over, and I'll run in and get us some.

Sue: Look, Bob, I think maybe Jeff's had enough. Remember, he's driving.

Jeff: Don't be stupid. The night is only beginning.

Bob: That's right. Jeff doesn't have any problem with alcohol. He can drink all night and stay in control.

Jeff pulls up to the curb. He and Bob get out and exit.

Sue: Linda, when you asked me along, you didn't tell me about all the drinking.

Linda: They just want to have a good time. Why don't you loosen up a little? I don't want them to think you're a jerk.

Sue: At this point, I really don't care what they think. This is not the kind of evening I had in mind. I thought we were going to the movies.

Linda: We will. Later. But now just go along with it. Bob is a really fun guy, if you'll just let him be himself.

Sue: What I'd like to do is find a phone and get a ride home.

Linda: Shhh. Here they come. They're going to hear you.

Jeff: (*Opening the door and handing a sack to* **Linda**.) A couple of six-packs for me and another bottle of our special elixir.

The car starts off as **Linda** *opens the sack and lifts out the bottle with one hand and a six-pack with the other.*

Linda: What will it be?

Bob: A couple of beers back here.

Sue: (*Turning to him.*) I told you, Bob, I don't drink.

Bob: It's only beer. You do drink beer, don't you?

Sue: No.

Bob: (*Shaking his head.*) I don't believe this.

Linda: Go on, Sue. It'll make the movie more fun.

Sue *shakes her head.*

Jeff: If she wants to be a wet blanket, let her.

Jeff *again drinks for several seconds without stopping. With his head back, he doesn't watch the road.*

Sue: Jeff, you just went through a stop sign.

Jeff: (*Shrugs.*) There was no one coming.

Linda: Maybe we'd better go to the park and stop. What if a cop saw you?

Jeff: Anything you say. You want to go to the park, we'll go to the park.

The lights fade to black.

Scene ii

The lights quickly come up once again to indicate the car has moved to the park. Bottles and cans litter the floor, front and back.

Jeff: That's it, huh? We should have gotten more.

Linda: Even you've had enough, Jeff. You really downed the booze.

Jeff: Don't you start too. Anyhow, I didn't see you pass anything up.

Sue: I think it'd be a good idea for me to drive to the movie.

Jeff: You're doubting my ability to drive?

Sue: I know you have enough alcohol in your bloodstream to make you legally drunk. If a cop stopped you, you'd be hauled off to jail.

Jeff: No one's going to drive this car but me. I can drive as well as ever.

Jeff pulls the car out onto the road. Suddenly, the two girls scream. Jeff quickly turns the wheel, swerving back and forth.

Sue: You didn't even see that truck!

Jeff: Sure, I did. He shouldn't have been there.

Sue: You could have killed us. I'm the one who should be driving.

Jeff: I told you. No one drives this car but me.

Sue: Then pull over at the service station. I want to get out.

Linda: Come on, Sue. We're almost at the movie. Just a few more minutes.

Sue: If Jeff insists on driving, I'm getting out.

Questions for Discussion

1. How did you feel about what Sue did?

2. Should Sue have gotten out of the car earlier?

3. Which person exerted the strongest peer pressure? What makes you think so?

4. Could Sue have handled the situation differently?

5. Which of the four persons do you most admire? Which do you admire the least? Why?

Peer Pressure to Take Drugs

The action takes place in the living room of Ryan's house. His parents are out of town for the weekend, and he has hosted a party. It is late, and most of the guests have gathered into smaller groups or left. **Ryan, Vicki, Tricia,** *and* **Grant** *are in a little room just off the living room.*

Ryan: Come on, Vicki, it's not going to kill you.

Tricia: Believe me, it'll do just the opposite. All your troubles will disappear.

Grant: They'll float away on a gentle breeze.

Vicki: I really don't think —

> **Ryan** *takes a drag on the marijuana cigarette and holds his breath.*

Grant: It's great stuff, you'll see. Once you try it, you'll wonder where it was all your life.

Tricia: You saw what Ryan did. You inhale and hold it, and pretty soon, your troubles seem far away.

149

Vicki: I've heard of people having bad trips.

> **Ryan** *passes the toke to* **Grant,** *who inhales deeply before passing it on to* **Tricia.**

Ryan: Not with grass, man. You're thinking of stronger stuff.

Vicki: No, I'm not. I've heard of people hallucinating, even one man who dived out of a high window.

> *As the action continues,* **Ryan, Tricia,** *and* **Grant** *pass the cigarette back and forth.*

Tricia: Even if that's true, which I very much doubt, it has to be the exception.

Ryan: (*Putting his arm around Vicki's shoulder and holding the roach to her lips.*) Come on, Vicki, you don't know what you're missing.

Tricia: You told me you were having troubles at home now, didn't you?

Vicki: (*Tentatively.*) Yeah.

Tricia: So make those troubles go away.

Vicki: You really think this is going to do that?

Grant: Maybe not make them go away. But make it so you don't care.

Tricia: Come on, Vicki.

Vicki: (*Starting to rise.*) I think I better go home.

Ryan: How are you going to get there, Vic?

Vicki: What?

Ryan: (*Laughing.*) I said, how are you going to get there? Now me, I might just fly, I feel so high. (*He laughs harder.*) Catch my rhyme? *I might just fly, 'cause I feel so high.* (*Peering closely at* Vicki.) But you're earthbound, baby. And it's too far to walk.

Vicki *sits back down.*

Ryan: That's better. I'm glad you're joining the party.

Tricia: You don't want to go home anyway. Not after the fight you had with your mom.

Vicki: I don't think—

Tricia: Believe me, you've never felt so good.

Vicki: Well...

Questions for Discussion

1. What is Vicki's first mistake?

2. What are some ways peer pressure can be positive?

3. Do you think Vicki's family problems contribute to her using marijuana?

4. What other choices can Vicki make?

Wanting to Get Off Drugs

The action takes place in a peer counseling class.

Barbara: You mean your father keeps marijuana in the house?

Leslie: Yes. He's been smoking pot since the '60s.

Tim: How do you feel about it?

Leslie: I grew up with it. It was no big deal. When dad's friends came over, they'd sit around and light up like they were having coffee together.

Barbara: What changed your mind?

Leslie: I got hooked. I started with marijuana and wound up a cocaine addict.

Barbara: I didn't know. Maybe I shouldn't have asked.

Leslie: It's OK. I wanted you all to know. I'll be out of school for a few weeks, and I didn't want you to wonder what happened.

Tim: Are you going somewhere?

Leslie: To a drug rehabilitation center. I want to kick my habit.

Barbara: That's great, Leslie. I know you'll be glad you did.

Tim: Afterwards, you're going to enjoy a lot more things. I'm speaking from experience. I've been sober six months, and I wonder how I lived like I did before.

Leslie: It took a long time to make my decision. And it wasn't easy to do. I had some great support.

Tim: I went kicking and screaming. My parents signed me in, and now I'm glad. At first, I was angry.

Leslie: If I left it up to my parents, I wouldn't be going. Dad won't admit he has a problem with drugs. And Mom just won't face any difficult issues.

Tim: Didn't you tell us once that you live with your dad? That your parents are divorced?

Leslie: Yeah. Mom lives in Arizona.

Tim: Will you go back with your Dad when you leave the rehab center?

Leslie: I shouldn't be in the same environment — where pot's available all the time. But I don't know where I'll go if I don't go home.

Barbara: You wouldn't want to live with your mom?

Leslie: If I wasn't a senior, sure. But I want to graduate here. I'll have a home teacher at the center, so I shouldn't get too far behind.

Tim: I don't know about you, Leslie, but I've never seen anyone strong enough to resist when they first got out. I mean, not if they go right back to the same environment.

Leslie: (*Sighs.*) I don't know if I have any other choices.

Tim: What about the social workers at the center? I'm sure they can help you figure something out.

Leslie: I hope so. I'll just take it a step at a time. Dad's insurance will cover the treatment, so he said I could go. So, next Monday, while you're all here in peer counseling, I'll be working on my own problems.

Tim: I got a lot of support from this class when I was getting off drugs. You'll find that out when you come back.

Leslie: That's why I wanted to tell everyone before I left.

Questions for Discussion

1. What personal characteristics does Leslie exhibit in referring herself to a drug treatment center?

2. What could the peer counseling class do to support her when she returns to class?

3. If Leslie's father continues to have marijuana in the house, would it be considered child abuse? Why or why not?

4. Because of Tim's background, he might be able to support Leslie in ways the other peer counselors can't. List some of these ways.

5. Discuss the pros and cons of Leslie's living with her mom or her dad after she returns from the treatment center. What place do you think would be better for her? Are there other alternatives? Make a list.

EATING DISORDERS

Having Bulimia

The action takes place in Janet's house. The time is one A.M. Six girls are sitting around a kitchen table, eating. A pizza box, soft drinks, and a donut box sit on the table.

Janet: (*Holding out a slice of pizza to* **Ashley**.) How about another piece?

Ashley: (*Reaching for the pizza.*) I shouldn't, but maybe just one more.

Lydia: What's a slumber party without eating lots of food?

Ann: Besides, Ashley, you don't have to worry. You're the thinnest person here. You always seem to be able to eat all you want without gaining.

Lydia: That's because she's a dancer. You know how dancers burn tons of calories. It's all those hours of practice. They're all pencil thin.

Janet: Come to think of it, Ashley, you used to talk about having to diet. But I haven't heard you mention the word in months.

Ashley: (*Finishes her pizza and reaches for a donut.* Don't worry about it. Let's just say I've found a better way of doing things.

Janet *looks at her quizzically.*

Ashley: Just don't worry about it. I'll take care of everything.

Janet: (*Deliberately changing the subject.*) Did you see that outfit Kelly wore to the football game?

Ashley *exits.*

Brenda: How could anyone miss it? I'd die to have something like that. Where does she find all those fantastic clothes?

Ellen: Her mother's a buyer at Neiman-Marcus. She gets them for her.

Brenda: It doesn't seem fair that one person has all the luck. Besides the clothes, she has the looks to go with them.

Janet: Did you notice that Ashley slipped out while we were talking about Kelly?

Lydia: I have noticed that she always seems to go to the bathroom as soon as she finishes eating.

Sue: I'm really worried about her. Particularly after what she said about "finding a better way."

Janet: Last week, a speaker in one of my classes at school talked about anorexia — and binging and purging.

Sue: I've heard of anorexia. But I don't know about...what did you call it? Binging and purging?

Brenda: It's eating a lot and then making yourself throw up.

Lydia: How disgusting!

Janet: The speaker said it can cause serious health problems if a person keeps on doing it.

Ashley: (*Standing in the kitchen doorway.*) Like what kind of problems?

Janet: Oh, hi, Ashley. We were just talking about a speaker I heard last week.

Ashley: I know. What kind of problems?

Janet: She said a person's body chemistry can be thrown off, and all kinds of organs affected. Like the heart. A person's teeth can even decay because of stomach acid.

Sue: I'm worried about you, Ashley. I didn't understand what you meant when you said you'd found a better way than dieting.

Janet: I think we're all concerned, Ashley. We're your friends, and we care about you.

Ashley: OK, OK. What if I do...what you think? It's no big deal.

Janet: That's just the point. Binging and purging *is* a big deal. It's dangerous.

Ashley: (*Sitting down at the table.*) But you don't understand. If I gain an ounce, I don't have a chance at any of the good roles at the dance theater. (*Pauses.*) I get so tired of not eating. I want to enjoy slumber parties and eat with the rest of you. Getting rid of my food just seems like a way to be one of the group and still stay at the weight I need for dancing. Maybe you can't understand. Maybe only other dancers can know.

Questions for Discussion

1. What are the symptoms of bulimia?

2. Are there certain groups of people who have a tendency to be bulimic? If so, which groups?

3. What health problems can be caused by binging and purging?

4. How can a peer counselor support someone who is bulimic?

5. What is the difference between anorexia and bulimia?

Being Overweight

The action takes place in Shauna's bedroom, where she and three of her friends are talking.

Shauna: I'm so excited. Eric asked me to the prom.

Alice: Way to go, Shauna. He's one of the cutest guys on campus.

Shauna: And a lot of fun, too.

Beth: Have you thought about a dress?

Shauna: Something royal blue maybe. Or bright red. What do you think?

Susie: Definitely the red. With Eric in a red cummerbund and tie with his black tux, you'll look great.

Susie: So, two of us have dates now, with two more to go. (*Turning to* **Alice**.) How about you, Alice? Any prospects?

Alice: Wanda's brother Bob wants to ask me. At least, that's what Wanda said.

Shauna: I know Bob. You two will have a lot of fun. He's a real sweetheart.

Susie: Now we need to work on a date for you, Beth.

Beth: Don't bother. I won't get asked — not last year, not this year, not any year.

Shauna: Oh, come on, Beth. Don't be so pessimistic. With the three of us working on it, you're as good as there.

Beth: I don't want you twisting some poor guy's arm.

Alice: What do you mean, "twist someone's arm"?

Beth: Boys don't want to be seen with fat girls.

Alice: Oh, come one, Beth. You're not fat.

Beth: Twenty pounds overweight. To a boy, that's fat.

Shauna: You're a lot of fun, Beth. Pretty, too.

Beth: Why kid myself? I'd only be disappointed. No one's asked me out all semester.

Shauna: That's a cop-out! It's not like you to give up without trying.

Beth: (*Sighs deeply.*) I've already tried. Being friendly. Tutoring football players. Volunteering at all kinds of events. Doing everything I could think of to get to know guys.

Shauna: And?

Beth: They treat me like a sister. And guys don't ask their sisters to the prom.

Shauna: It's four weeks away. A lot can happen.

Beth: But it won't.

Shauna: You've got to believe in yourself. If you don't, no one else will.

Alice: That's true. Confidence shows.

Beth: But you're all so thin. That kind of thing will work for you. Being fat is like having the plague.

Susie: I know how you feel.

Beth *looks at her inquisitively.*

Susie: I was overweight till the beginning of my junior year.

Alice: When you moved here, you weren't.

Susie: When I found out we had to move, I made up my mind to lose all that extra fat. I worked hard all summer, and I mean hard — twenty laps a day in the pool, three miles of jogging, an hour in the gym. Plus a one-thousand calorie diet. I lost twenty-five pounds.

Shauna: And you haven't gained any back.

Susie: Perish the thought! I worked too hard to get it off. I watch what I eat, and I exercise. I feel a lot better about myself. And I do understand how you feel, Beth.

Beth: I never knew you had a weight problem.

Susie: All during junior high and the first two years of high school. I got sick of people always telling me what I should do to get thin. But I had to get motivated myself, or I'd never have lost those twenty-five pounds.

Beth: Maybe I've been working too hard at being accepted the way I am. I can't lose enough in time for the prom. But I'll bet I can lose twenty pounds by graduation.

Questions for Discussion

1. List the physical and emotional problems that may result from being overweight.

2. Beth says she may be working too hard on being accepted as she is rather than working on her weight problem. Discuss this situation. Is your conclusion the same as hers, or is it different?

3. Beth doesn't expect to be asked to the prom, but all her friends are going. Describe what you think her real feelings are.

4. Susie says she became motivated to lose weight. Discuss how a peer counselor can help a counselee become motivated to accomplish a goal.

5. Beth seems to doubt her own level of confidence. Discuss ways of helping someone become more confident.

Being Anorexic

The action occurs in a small restaurant. **Ginny** *and* **Jessica** *sit at a booth.*

Ginny: (*Glancing at a menu.*) What looks good to you, Jess?

Jessica: Nothing, really. I don't think I'll have anything.

Ginny: Nothing?

Jessica: Maybe just a glass of water.

Ginny: Look, Jessica, we've been friends for a long time, and I'm getting really worried about you.

Jessica: Why's that?

Ginny: I've watched you lose weight now for more than six months.

Jessica: You and I agreed on a diet. What's the problem?

Ginny: You're right. We agreed to go on a diet together. But not to keep on it till we were as thin as rails.

Jessica: Who's thin as a rail?

Ginny: *You* are!

Jessica: I don't agree. In fact, I need to lose more.

Ginny: Jess, look at me. I wanted to lose ten pounds, and I did. Now I'm back eating regular meals.

Jessica: You look great.

Ginny: You could, too — if you'd put a few pounds back on.

Jessica: What do you mean? You don't want to gain back your weight.

Ginny: I'm not as thin as you. I stopped dieting — you didn't.

Jessica: I think I need to lose more. Ginny, when I look in the mirror, I see how fat I still am.

Ginny: A few weeks ago, I wouldn't have been able to talk about this. But now, I think I understand what's happening.

Jessica: What do you mean?

Ginny: I'm in a peer counseling class where we have speakers tell us about all kinds of problems.

Jessica: What does that have to do with me?

Ginny: Last week a woman at school talked to us about eating disorders. Anorexia and bulimia.

Jessica: I had a friend who was anorexic. She had to go into the hospital.

Ginny: I know. It can be really serious.

Jessica: You don't mean you think I'm anorexic.

Ginny: I don't know, Jess. Your symptoms seem to fit.

Jessica: What symptoms?

Ginny: Thinking you still need to lose when you're already too thin.

Jessica: Do you really think I'm too thin?

Ginny: Just look at your clothes. They hang on you. Even the things your mother bought you last month are too loose.

Jessica: Mom said the same thing. I think she's getting concerned.

Ginny: Then don't you think you need to start eating again?

Jessica: If I were hungry, I'd eat. But I'm not. I've lost all interest in food.

Ginny: Doesn't that worry you?

Jessica: Not when I think I still need to lose. If a glass of water satisfies me, why not pass up the food till I get my weight where I want it?

Ginny: Jess, you haven't heard a word I've said.

Jessica: I have. But I don't agree.

Ginny: And that's the problem. You don't see yourself the way you are. You sincerely think you need to continue losing. Isn't that kind of scary?

Jessica: You think I really have a problem?

Ginny: Yes.

Jessica: What do you think I should do?

Ginny: In peer counseling, we learn that we're not supposed to give advice. But I haven't completed the course. I'm not a real peer counselor yet. Anyway, you're my best friend, and we've always told each other what we think. Look, Jess, I think you need to get help. You need to talk to an expert, like the woman who came to our class. I'll bet your mom would take you to see her.

Jessica: But when I look in the mirror, I really don't think I look thin enough. Really, Ginny, I don't.

Questions for Discussion

1. What are some symptoms of anorexia? Compare those symptoms to what you read about Jessica.

2. Does Ginny have good reason to be worried about Jessica? Why or why not?

3. What else could Ginny do to help Jessica understand her problem?

4. Is Ginny a good peer counselor? Why or why not?

5. Compare Ginny and Jessica's dieting. What are the differences?

GANGS

Territorial Rights

The action occurs in a high school
peer counseling class.

Brenda: He just wanted to fit in. And now he's dead. All because of territory.

Margaret: Wow! I'm sorry.

Brenda: I couldn't believe it.

Margaret: Everything you're telling us is...it's like it's from another world or something. I mean, I've never even met anyone before who lived where there were gangs. I don't know anything about them, except what I see on TV.

Brenda: (*Shaking her head.*) You don't know how lucky you are not to have gangs here.

Jeff: All this happened only a few miles away? It's hard to believe.

Margaret: I'm glad Mary brought you today. But doesn't it seem strange? You two are cousins, and your lives have been so different.

Brenda: I guess I've been pretty bitter about that. You know, why did we have to live in that area? If we'd lived somewhere else...

Sally: You said you and Brian grew up in the same neighborhood?

Brenda: I knew him all my life. A really nice guy. Sensitive. He wanted to be a writer.

Sally: Since you knew each other so well, did he tell you when he joined the gang?

Brenda: Not really. I knew he wanted to be accepted, to fit in.

Sally: I can understand that. I think everyone wants to belong.

Brenda: Well, he hung out with some of the guys. I was on the fringes. I hadn't been initiated. And maybe because of my own feelings, I thought Brian never joined either.

Candy: I think you've left us kind of speechless.

Brenda: I don't understand.

Candy: You don't fit the image. (*Shakes her head.*) What I mean is, I've always thought of girls who travel with gangs as different. Tough-acting, maybe. Street smart, but you don't seem much different than any of us.

Brenda: Maybe not. But I assure you, there are differences. None of you has ever seen the kind of things I have. Not just what happened to Brian, but all kinds of other things, too.

Tony: I'm not sure I follow that.

Brenda: Violence, for one thing. You've got to understand where these people are coming from. The gang members. Most of them feel left out, like they don't have anything. So when they want things, they go after them. They don't see any point in working their butts off to get them. Why do that, they figure, when they can rip things off? Car stereos or whatever.

Tony: But some of them are bound to get caught.

Brenda: Sure, and the kids I know have been really sorry about that. There was this one guy who stole a stereo from a car. He'd been a gang member only a month. You know what he said? "I sacrificed seven months of freedom for a stereo."

Sally: But some of them do it again, don't they? As soon as they get out.

Brenda: A lot of them do. They go to the youth authority camp for months at a time, even kids who haven't been in trouble before. And they meet these guys who are older, tougher, more experienced. And they pick up their attitudes and ideas. Some of them do try to go straight, though.

Margaret: You were going to tell us about...your boyfriend. About Brian.

Brenda: He was never into violence. Never into heavy stuff at all.

Jeff: Then how...?

Brenda: How did he die?

Jeff *nods.*

Brenda: It was a payback. It involved this thing about territory.

Margaret: I don't know what that means. A "payback?"

Brenda: A week before he was shot, Brian and some of the other guys from the gang were cruising the neighborhood after a movie. They crossed into a rival gang's territory. That's it. The other gang thought they shouldn't be there. So this rival gang jumped them at a red light.

Jeff: But Brian wasn't killed then.

Brenda: No. There were enough guys in the car to be able to defend themselves. But before they took off, Brian hit one of the other gang members. Really hurt him, I guess.

Jeff: And the payback was for hurting this guy?

Brenda: Yes, but it wasn't fair. Brian was riding his bike home from work, minding his own business, in his own territory. A car drove by, and someone fired a gun. Someone from the other gang. Brian didn't have a chance. (*Crying.*) They shot him full of holes. He was dead before he even knew what happened.

Sally: How awful.

Brenda: My life will never be the same. Part of me died with him.

Questions for Discussion

1. Why is it important to have visitors such as Brenda come to the peer counseling class?

2. What do you think Brenda felt visiting a school so different from hers?

3. Candy is surprised that Brenda didn't fit the stereotype of a gang member. Discuss the ways preconceptions affect how we relate to other people.

4. Brenda says her boyfriend wanted a place to fit in. What alternatives did he have?

5. Why do you think Brenda didn't join the gang?

Invitation to Join

The action takes place at Sam's house. **Sam** *and*
Ralph *are working on Ralph's motorcycle.*

Ralph: I've seen what gangs can do to people. I don't want any part of it.

Sam: It feels good to belong, to be accepted. Like you're part of something big.

Ralph: You don't need to be to be in a gang to be somebody. You can just be yourself and be somebody.

Sam: Then why wasn't I somebody before I joined? I was never a part of anything at school. I was always lonely.

Ralph: I don't know. Maybe you didn't believe in yourself. Maybe you didn't try to make friends.

Sam: Oh, yeah, I tried. But it was no good. And I couldn't take it. Especially after Dad died. Mom had to work two shifts at the hospital just to make enough to live on. So I never saw her or anyone else. If I'd had just one person to talk to... But there was no one. You understand? No one.

Ralph: That must have been rough.

Sam: Yeah, but then Brian came along and asked me to join.

Ralph: Weren't you scared? I've heard some pretty bad things about the initiation.

Sam: You mean getting "jumped in."

Ralph: I guess so. If that's the initiation.

Sam: It shows you can take it.

Ralph: Take what?

Sam: The beating. The members all get to beat you up. But once you're in, that's it. You get to give it to the next guy.

Ralph: It doesn't sound like fun to me. Does anyone ever get hurt? Really bad, I mean.

Sam: You know the saying, "If you want in the gang, you have to take the pain."

Ralph: What if you want out?

Sam: Same thing.

Ralph: What do you mean?

Sam: You get "jumped out."

Ralph: Another beating?

Sam: Right. But this one's worse, 'cause anything goes.

Ralph: That's not for me. I wouldn't want to get into anything like that.

Sam: There are other ways to get out. You can get religion, or you can move. At least, that's the way it is with our gang. If you want to do religious work, you can leave without being jumped out.

Ralph: And if you move?

Sam: Your gang is your family. If you leave, it's like going AWOL. If they ever find you, you could be in big trouble. But usually they don't try.

Ralph: Since I'm new here, I'd like to make friends. But I don't want to join any gang. I don't need something like that, you understand what I'm saying? I can make it on my own.

Sam: Whatever you say.

Questions for Discussion

1. Why do you think Ralph is so confident?

2. Do you think he will remain confident in his new neighborhood, or will he join the gang later?

3. Sam says he was very lonely before joining the gang. List some characteristics of loneliness and discuss ways to combat them.

4. What could Sam have done to raise his self-esteem?

5. Do you think it will be possible for Ralph and Sam to still be friends? Why or why not?

A New Start

The action occurs in a peer counseling class.

Sam: There's something I've been wanting to tell you, but I haven't. I'm scared.

Terry: We won't tell anyone. Everything here's confidential.

Sam: I'm worried what you'll think. About something I've done. Before I moved here, I mean.

Julie: Everyone thinks you're an OK guy, Sam. Right? (*She glances around the class as others nod in agreement.*) You couldn't tell us anything that would make us feel differently.

Sam: I know I've been accepted here. But that makes it worse. I'm more hesitant than ever to tell you what this is about.

Terry: It's up to you. We'll be glad to listen. It's kind of like we're all one big family.

Sam: (*Taking a deep breath.*) At my other school, I belonged to a family too. A different kind.

Julie: Like a team or something?

Sam: (*Deciding to take the plunge.*) I belonged to a gang.

There is a moment of silence.

Terry: What about it, Sam?

Sam: I'm not very proud of the things we did.

Terry: But that was last year. You're out of it now.

Sam: Thanks to my parents. My dad took a cut in pay just so we could move.

Julie: They must care a lot about you.

Sam: Yeah. A friend of mine, the guy who got me to join the gang, was killed. That's when my parents started talking about moving. They could see the death really shook me up. I mean, he was a great guy. And they were worried about me, too.

Julie: So your folks checked and found out there are no gangs here.

Sam: (*Nods.*) They looked at the school pretty carefully. But you know what? Even if there were gangs here, I wouldn't be a member. I wasn't strong enough back then to stick it out on my own. But I'm sure I am now.

Julie: What do you think's made the difference?

Sam: Last year, I was lonely. All the time. I had no friends, so I needed to belong to something. It turned out to be the gang. (*He smiles and glances at the other class members.*) Here it was easier to make friends. Mainly because of this class.

Julie: Maybe we're all different, but everyone has a need to belong.

Questions for Discussion

1. Why do you think Sam wanted to share his past with his peer counseling class?

2. Do you think Sam's parents did the right think in moving to another neighborhood?

3. Describe how it feels to belong. What things do people do in order to belong?

4. Discuss ways peer counselors can help new students feel that they belong.

5. What makes students in peer counseling feel their class is a family? What conditions would keep them from feeling that way?

HOME LIFE

Throwaway Kids

The action occurs just after school. **Jerry** *has stopped in at* **Phil's** *house. The boys, who are both sixteen, work at a nearby restaurant.* **Phil** *is sitting on the bed in his room, changing his shoes.* **Jerry** *stands by the window.*

Phil: You look beat, Jerry.

Jerry: (*Turning to face* **Phil.**) You could say that.

Phil: What's the matter?

Jerry: (*Shrugs and starts to turn away.*) Nothing.

Phil: (*Standing up.*) Hey, it's me, man. Haven't we been friends since second grade? Something's bothering you, I can tell.

Jerry: Can you?

Phil: Yeah, I can. So out with it. Nothing can be that bad.

Jerry: I didn't want to tell you, but I can't— (*His voice breaks.*) My mom kicked me out. She kicked me out and told me not to come back.

Phil: Did you have a fight or something?

Jerry: (*He shakes his head.*) It's for good, man. You know, like forever. I can't even get my clothes.

Phil: Why?

Jerry: It's her husband. (*He sighs.*) She got married last month, you know. And John, the guy she married, said it was either him or me.

Phil: I thought you liked him.

Jerry: Not much. I pretended I did so it wouldn't make Mom feel bad. I mean, Dad's been dead for almost three years now, and she had a heck of a struggle raising me and Becky. I thought she deserved...

Phil: So what are you going to do?

Jerry: I don't know. I really don't.

Phil: When did all this happen?

Jerry: Yesterday, when I got home from school. I didn't have to work. It was one of my evenings off. (**Jerry** sits on the edge of the bed.) She didn't even let me inside.

Phil: I don't know what to say. I'm... I'm sorry.

Jerry: (*Looking up at him.*) Not half as sorry as I am.

Phil: Just like that, she kicked you out? What did she say?

Jerry: What could she say? She was crying. She said John told her she had put it off long enough. If he came home and found me there, he said he was packing his bags.

Phil: (*Sitting beside* **Jerry.**) What about your sister?

Jerry: Mom told me she could stay, but she couldn't have any contact with me or say anything about it, or she gets trashed as well.

Phil: What are you going to do?

Jerry: I don't know. I thought she loved me. I thought we got along OK, as much as anyone does. We've never been in trouble, my sister or me. Nothing serious.

Phil: I know. (*Suddenly,* **Phil** *looks at* **Jerry**.) Where did you spend the night?

Jerry: Mostly walking, trying to figure things out. But trying to ignore what happened. Pretending I'd lost my key or something and nobody else was home. (*Pause.*) I hung around the bowling alley for awhile, then went to the bus station and sat on one of the benches. I had about twenty bucks from my last paycheck, so later I went to Denny's. If anyone looked my way, I acted like I was reading the paper.

Phil: What are you going to do?

Jerry: I always had this dumb dream. I wanted to be a teacher, like Mr. Long, you remember? Junior high P.E.? He was a good guy, 'cause you could tell he really cared. I wanted to be like him. I knew Mom couldn't help very much, but I figured I'd get through college on my own, somehow. (*He stands up and walks to the bedroom window.*) Not much of a dream, was it?

Phil: Is there anything I can do to help?

Jerry: Naw. I've got to quit school, that's for sure. Get a full-time job. I was going to talk to the manager today, at the restaurant.

Phil: Why don't you stay here tonight, Jer? I'm sure it would be OK with Mom and Dad.

Jerry: Then what? Yeah, I appreciate the offer. But it's my whole life, man, not just one night. (*He turns and half leans, half sits on the window sill.*) I thought, maybe, I could stay at Tom's a couple of nights, and maybe at Annie's, if it's OK with her parents. And yeah, a couple of nights with you. (*He laughs bitterly.*) Don't want to over-stay any welcome. I don't want to get kicked out again.

Phil: We'll work things out. Maybe the other kids will have some ideas. The first thing is to let them all know.

Jerry: It's like...like something shameful. Like I don't want anyone to know. I know that's dumb, but I can't help feeling that way.

Phil: All those kids. Runaways, throwaways. You hear about them. But it's like it doesn't affect you. It's someone else. You never think it can happen to someone you know. Someone you've known all your life.

Questions for Discussion

1. Have you known someone who has been kicked out of his or her house? What were some of the feelings they expressed?

2. What are some of Jerry's options?

3. As a peer counselor, would you need to report Jerry's situation as child abuse?

4. How do you think Jerry's mother feels about the situation?

5. Why do you think Jerry's stepfather wants him out of the house, but allows Jerry's sister to remain?

6. What risk did Jerry take by not being honest with his mother about his feelings toward his prospective step-father?

Runaway Kids

The action takes place outside a movie theatre at a large mall. **Joette** *and* **Kathy** *are leaning against the wall.*

Joette: I think you're making a big mistake. No matter what it's like at home, it's better to wait till you finish school. Then take off if you want to.

Kathy: You don't understand. I hate this place. It's not only my mom and dad. It's everything.

Joette: What do you mean? I thought you just didn't get along with your folks.

Kathy: Yeah, there's that. But I can't trust anyone. All my friends are two-faced. They'd rather gossip than anything else. Like Liz. I thought she was my friend, so I told her some things about Tom and me. Things she had no business telling anyone else. The next thing you know, it's all over school.

Joette: Won't it just blow over?

Kathy: I don't like what people say about me behind my back. If they have something to say, why don't they come out and say it?

Joette: But is it worth running away? You know that film we saw at school. About all those street kids. They're passed from one guy to another, and a lot of them have AIDS.

Kathy: It won't be like that for me. I'll get a job. I'll do OK.

Joette: What kind of job? What can you do, Kathy? You can work at a fast-food place, but that's minimum wage. You can't make it on that. Where will you stay?

Kathy: I'll work it out, don't worry.

Joette: A lot of people care about you, Kathy. They really do.

Kathy: Yeah, sure. Like I said, you think they're your friends, but they all turn on you.

Joette: Do you have any money?

Kathy: Yeah, I do. Five or six hundred, from my job. I was saving it to buy a car.

Joette: How long do you think that will last, Kathy? Not very long.

Kathy: Hey, I don't know why you're butting in. I didn't ask you.

Joette: You said you don't have friends. That's wrong. I care about you. You've got a lot going for you.

Kathy: Then you're the only one. (*Glances up.*) Look, here's Carl. You remember.

Carl *strides up to the two girls.*

Carl: Hi, Kath. What's up?

Kathy: Hi, Carl. You remember Joette?

Carl: Yeah. You sat right behind me in sophomore English.

Joette: Hi, Carl. So, how have you been?

Carl: I get by. It's a hard, cruel world, in case you haven't heard.

Joette: I suppose it is.

Kathy: So tell her, Carl. She's worried I won't make it. I told her you said you'd show me the ropes. How to get by.

Carl: I'm a master at that.

Joette: So, what are you doing now, Carl?

Carl: Working in a gas station. Me and three other guys share an apartment.

Kathy: You didn't tell me that. When did you move in?

Carl: It's not much. Just one bedroom. But, till something better comes along...

Joette: I was trying to talk Kathy into waiting till she finishes school to get away.

Carl: Sometimes the world keeps coming down on you. You can't wait.

Joette: Maybe it's a little easier for a boy, don't you think? I mean, I've heard all the stories.

Carl: Yeah, OK. Probably what you've heard is true.

Kathy: I won't have it so rough. The money will last me. I'll get a job. (*She looks at* **Joette**.) I can stay at Carl's place if it comes right down to it, can't I?

Carl: No room, babe. I'm sorry.

Kathy: (*Angry.*) I might have known. You're just like everyone else. Well, I don't need you. I don't need anybody. Maybe I'll see you around. (*She turns and half runs, half walks away.*)

Joette: Kathy, wait, please wait, I think you're making a big mistake. (**Kathy** *continues walking.*) A big mistake!

Carl: (*Shrugs, grins, and walks away. He turns back toward* **Joette**.) Hey, Joette, lighten up. She'll be OK.

Questions for Discussion

1. Describe your idea of Kathy's home. Why would she run away?

2. Why does Kathy feel she doesn't have any friends?

3. Name some of the dangers Kathy faces.

4. Can Joette do anything differently to convince Kathy to remain at home?

5. Joette says it might be a little easier for a boy to be on his own. Do you agree or disagree? Why?

Having Added Responsibility

The action occurs at lunchtime. **Joanne** *and* **Phyllis**
are standing by their lockers.

Joanne: So, anyhow, I'm in a real bind. It may come down to my having to quit school.

Phyllis: This close to graduation? That would be awful.

Joanne: I just can't keep up. Besides working at my job, which I really need now that Mom's in the hospital, I have to do all the housework and take care of my brother and sister.

Phyllis: I wish there was something I could do. Any idea how long this is going to go on?

Joanne: Mom's operation is scheduled for next Monday. But even when she comes home, she's not supposed to do much for at least a couple of months.

Phyllis: What about during the day, when you're in school?

Joanne: That's one of the reasons I think I'll have to quit school. I hate to leave Mom alone.

Phyllis: Have you talked to any of the teachers?

Joanne: What can they do?

Phyllis: How about someone in the counseling office? Maybe they can help.

Joanne: How? I just can't keep up. As it is, I'll have to get my work hours changed so I can be at home when the kids get there. They're only six and seven years old.

Phyllis: What about relatives? Can they help?

Joanne: My dad took off a couple of years ago. And Mom's family is way on the other side of the country.

Phyllis: I don't see how you can handle all this.

Joanne: (*Starts to cry.*) I don't know either. It's really getting to be too much for me.

Phyllis: Maybe there's some way you could keep up with your lessons.

Joanne: It's a nice idea, Phyllis. But I'd be so far behind. And we need the money from my job.

Phyllis: Can't your mom get unemployment or workman's compensation or something like that?

Joanne: Don't you think we've tried everything? She's just lucky to have hospitalization insurance. At least that'll be taken care of. But there are still the utilities, the groceries, the rent. I don't know what I'm going to do.

Phyllis: Do you go to a church? Could people help you there?

Joanne: Mom's never been very religious. And anyhow, you know how it is. Remember when Billy Jenkins had leukemia, and we were all going to visit him? After a couple of weeks no one ever went.

Phyllis: I guess I'm one of the guilty ones. I had good intentions.

Joanne: But you're human. We all have good intentions.

Phyllis: Will you let me try to help? To see what I can do?

Joanne: (*Shrugs.*) I appreciate your wanting to help. But what can you do?

Phyllis: First, let me talk to some of the teachers and maybe some other people. OK?

Joanne: If you want to.

Questions for Discussion

1. We do not know if Phyllis is a peer counselor. Do you think she is? Why or why not?

2. Joanne seems very willing to assume responsibility for the family. What qualities do you think she has that make her so responsible?

3. Should Phyllis talk to the teacher and other persons on Joanne's behalf? Why or why not?

4. If you were the peer counselor, list some places to which you would refer Joanne.

5. Is Joanne being realistic by taking on all the responsibilities by herself?

6. What do you think about Joanne postponing school for a semester?

Staying Out Late

Scene i

The scene is the living room of the Goodman house. It is late afternoon.

Jean: Mom, I just want to stay out till two, that's all. One night. I won't ask again. It's a special dance. All my friends are going.

Mom: When you're eighteen and on your own, you can stay out as late as you want. But while you're living in this house, you'll obey the rules.

Jean: Come on, Mom. What will the other kids think?

Mom: I don't care what they think.

Jean: I'll be with Bob, Linda, Toni, Sam, and —

Mom: No, Jean, I'm not going to change my mind.

Jean: You can trust them. You know you can.

Mom: I'm not going to get into an argument with you. You'll be home on time, and that's that.

Jean: What if I don't come home? You can't do anything about it.

Mom: We'll see.

Jean: What will you do, ground me? That won't work. You can't force me to stay here. You can't lock me in my room. I'll do what I please.

Mom: I don't know what's come over you.

Jean: I'm not a kid anymore, Mom. I can take care of myself.

Mom: No matter what happens?

Jean: I think so.

Mom: That's something you'll have to prove.

Jean: You're not giving me the chance.

Mom: I don't see you behaving very responsibly.

Jean: Well, I'm going to stay out as long as I want. And that's that.

Blackout.

Scene ii

The lights come up on a booth in a restaurant. **Jean** *is seated with a group of friends, those with whom she wants to go to the dance. Her boyfriend is* **Sam.**

Sam: So what did your mom say? Is it OK?

Jean: Don't worry. Everything's taken care of. I'll stay out as long as I want.

Sam: Your mom said it was OK?

Jean: As a matter of fact, she didn't. But what's she going to do? Lock me in a closet for the rest of my life?

Sam: Well, it's up to you, but...

Jean: But what, Sam?

Sam: If you can't stay out that late, I understand. Your curfew's 12:30 on weekends, right?

Jean: (*With exasperation.*) Right. What is this, anyhow? Are you siding with my mother?

Sam: I didn't think I was siding with anyone. I was thinking of you, that's all.

Linda: If she wants to stay out late, let her. What the heck? My mom doesn't care how late I stay out. Most of the time on weekends, she's not home anyway.

Sam: You can stay out as long as you like?

Linda: I sure can. Mom doesn't care.

Jean: You're lucky.

Linda: Am I?

Jean: You obviously have parents who understand.

Linda: A mother, anyhow.

Jean: OK, a mother then. Who lets you do as you please. Who gives you a lot of freedom.

Linda: Oh, yeah, she gives me a lot of freedom. (*Her voice becomes hard.*) All the freedom I want.

Jean: Linda?

Linda: Yeah, what is it?

Jean: Is something wrong?

Linda: You know, in a way I think you're the lucky one. You're important to your mother. She obviously cares for you.

Blackout.

Scene iii

The lights come up once more in the Goodman living room. **Sam** *has come to pick up* **Jean** *for the dance.*

Mom: Remember, Jean, I expect you home at 12:30. Not a second later.

Jean: Oh, Mom.

Mom: You'll see to it, won't you, Sam?

Sam: I'm try my best, Mrs. Goodman.

Jean: (*Kissing her mom on the cheek.*) 'Bye, Mom.

Mom: Remember what I said.

Jean: (*As she and* **Sam** *exit.*) We'll see, Mom. We'll see.

Questions for Discussion

1. Discuss more positive strategies Jean could have used to approach her mother about staying out late.

2. Jean's mom says, "You'll be home on time, and that's that." Name some less combative ways she could use to get her point across.

3. Linda seems to want some boundaries in her life. Discuss how important boundaries are for high school students.

4. Jean's mother asks Sam to get Jean home on time. Do you think it is Jean's or Sam's responsibility to see that Jean gets home on time?

5. The outcome is not known, but pretend that Jean does get home on time. Discuss the pros and cons. Now pretend she comes home late. Discuss the pros and cons of this. Make a comparison of the two outcomes.

Living in a Group Home

The action takes place in a peer counseling class.
Everyone is seated in a circle.

Carmen: I get to see my parents once a month. We can't be together more than an hour before we start fighting.

Sam: Is that the reason you're living at the Cameron House instead of at home?

Carmen: That's part of it. The real reason is that I ran away from home so many times.

Helen: You ran away?

Carmen: My parents didn't want me there, so we always fought. But whenever I'd leave, they'd call the police and get me picked up. They didn't want me, but they didn't want me to go either.

Sam: Sounds like a difficult spot to be in.

Carmen: "Difficult" isn't the word. Living at home was utter chaos.

Helen: Was it always like that?

Carmen: As long as I can remember. Mom's an alcoholic, drunk half the time. Dad's a truck driver, and he's almost never home, which is better for everyone.

Sam: I'd think with your mother's drinking, it might be better to have him home more often.

Carmen: You don't know my father. He has a bad temper. When he's mad, he beats up the first one he sees.

Sam: Even your mother?

Carmen: Mainly my mother, because she's there most of the time. My little brother and I always tried to stay away when we knew Dad was home.

Helen: Do you think your mother's drinking is related to being beaten?

Carmen: Probably at the beginning. My dad would drive anyone to drink. But now I think she's addicted. She drinks whether he's there or not.

Helen: I remember once you mentioned having two sisters.

Carmen *nods.*

Helen: They don't live at home?

Carmen: One ran away at fifteen and never came back.

Pam: Your parents didn't send the police after her?

Carmen: No, she wasn't Dad's kid. Mom had her before they were married. I think he was glad she left.

Pam: And your other sister? Is she your dad's daughter?

Carmen: Yes, but she got pregnant. She married her boyfriend and moved out.

Sam: So you were the last girl left at home?

Carmen: Yeah. I think that's why they kept coming after me when I left. They needed me to look after things.

Sam: You mean, to look after your brother?

Carmen: That and do the housework. If the house was a mess when Dad came home, I really caught it. It was like I was the maid. Like I said, I helped with my brother, too. And I always stuck up for him.

Pam: Are you worried, now that he's there without you?

Carmen: I think about him a lot. I really miss him.

Pam: Do you get to see him?

Carmen: About once a month.

Pam: That's nice.

Carmen: It sure is. We always talk about what we're going to do when I turn eighteen.

Helen: You're seventeen now?

Carmen: I'll be eighteen in nine months. Then I'm leaving Cameron House and getting a full-time job. I'll find a place to live, then I'll go get my brother.

Helen: That's an ambitious goal. You'll still be in high school, won't you?

Sam: Can't you stay at Cameron House till you graduate?

Carmen: Yeah. But I'm counting the months till I can get out.

Helen: I thought you liked it.

Carmen: I do. It's better than being home. But the restrictions get in the way.

Pam: What do you mean?

Carmen: Like we all have chores, like dusting, dishes, or whatever. We have room check at ten every night. That means I can't take the job I applied for at the movie theatre. I wouldn't get off till eleven. Then, too, I can leave Cameron House only one weekend a month. It gets in the way of my freedom.

Helen: Most of us have rules at home, too. I know I certainly do. But they're meant for my good.

Carmen: Probably for me too. (*Shrugs.*) I don't want you to think that Cameron House isn't a good place to live. It is. I've never had anyone treat me nice before. To the housemother, we're all her own kids. But I'm not used to rules. When Dad was gone, Mom never knew when I got in at night. I was pretty much a free spirit.

Helen: I can understand. I've rebelled against rules myself. But have you thought about how much easier it might be to take care of your brother if you had a diploma and could earn more money?

Carmen: Yeah, I've thought about it. I have to see a shrink each week. All the kids do. I didn't like it at first, but now it's OK. She's helped me get in touch with my feelings. I've found out that kids of alcoholics have a lot to deal with. And there are lots of us. It's comforting to know I'm not alone.

Sam: It sounds like Cameron House is a good place to be for now.

Carmen: I suppose. It's just all the rules I don't like.

Questions for Discussion

1. Carmen says that children of alcoholics have a lot of problems. What are some of them?

2. Why do you think Carmen's parents did not want her to leave home?

3. What are some things Carmen could do to make her adjustment in a group home easier?

4. Carmen mentions that she wants to help her brother, but she does not say anything about helping her mother. Why do you think she doesn't?

5. What would be the pros and cons of Carmen's leaving the group home before graduation?

Needing Love

The action occurs in the Dombrowski's living room.
Dad *has just returned from an overnight trip. After a few moments,* **Kathleen** *enters.*

Dad: Hi, honey.

Kathleen: Dad, I need to talk to you.

Dad: What is it?

Kathleen: Bonnie O.D.'d on drugs last night.

Dad: What?

Kathleen: She's in the hospital, in intensive care.

Dad: (*Sitting down.*) What happened?

Kathleen: That's the thing. She took Grandpa's pills.

Dad: What do you mean? What pills?

Kathleen: His Fiorinal.

Dad: I knew he couldn't find them. But that was a couple of weeks ago.

Kathleen: She'd been planning this for a long, long time.

Dad: Why?

Kathleen: Because of Jeff. You know how she is about Jeff. She's completely crazy when it comes to him. She keeps calling him and taking the bus to his house. He doesn't want anything to do with her.

Dad: How is she? Do you know?

Kathleen: Not very good. She took quite a few of the Fiorinal pills and some Tylenols too.

Dad: How did you find this out?

Kathleen: She was over here.

Dad: You better start at the beginning.

Kathleen: She came over and said she wanted to lie down on my bed. I said OK. I didn't think anything about it. You know she and her dad always fight. I thought she just wanted to get away.

Dad: She'd already taken the pills?

Kathleen: Yes. She was here a couple of hours, and Liz went in to get her up. Bonnie acted all dumb.

Dad: What do you mean?

Kathleen: Like she couldn't talk right, and she kept falling into the wall. And then she vomited all over my bed. We got her up and took her to the bathroom. After we went back to the living room, we heard a thump. We went to the bathroom and found her on the floor, almost unconscious.

Dad: Did you call her father?

Kathleen: She didn't want to see him. She said she just wanted Jeff. If she couldn't have him, she didn't want anything. She just went on and on about how she loved him.

Dad: So what happened?

Kathleen: Liz and I took Bonnie home, and her dad put her to bed. We had to take her home. We didn't know what else to do.

Dad: Didn't he take her to a hospital or call an ambulance?

Kathleen: No. He said he thought she'd be OK.

Dad: Couldn't he see the state she was in?

Kathleen: I guess not. I don't know. Anyhow she started having convulsions. Then he called for an ambulance. They came and took her to Memorial.

Dad: Poor kid.

Kathleen: It's her own fault. I tried to tell her to forget about Jeff.

Dad: Don't be too hard on her, Kathleen. Maybe her home life is bad. She might have needed someone to turn to. Maybe this was just her way of asking for help.

Kathleen: I don't know. She left a note but made sure it wouldn't be found right away.

Dad: How do you know that?

Kathleen: It was in a folder under her purse. I guess she figured no one would look there right away. (*Shrugs.*) She said she needed someone to love her. And if no one did, she wanted to die. She wrote what she'd taken, and how many of each kind. The last sentence just trails off, like she was too tired or too far gone on the pills to finish.

Dad: I certainly hope she'll be OK.

Kathleen: As soon as she's better physically, they're sending her to Mesa Verde, a psychiatric hospital south of town.

Questions for Discussion

1. Bonnie's note says she needed someone to love her. Discuss the importance of love in people's lives.

2. Do you think Bonnie communicated well with Jeff? Why or why not?

3. What other options did Bonnie have? Do you think she thought she had any? Why do you think she chose to attempt suicide?

4. What conditions in Bonnie's life put her at risk for suicide?

5. Was Bonnie's father negligent in not taking her to the hospital earlier? Discuss feelings that he might have been having.

HOMOSEXUALITY

Homosexual Student

The action occurs in the high school auditorium just after the dismissal bell has rung. **Tark** *and* **Dianne** *sit in the front row. They've come to help the dramatic arts teacher erect the set for the senior play. They're early because* **Tark** *has told* **Dianne,** *a long-time friend, that he needs to talk.*

Tark: You're taking that class, right? Where kids talk about their problems. Where they try to help each other.

Dianne: That's right. Mostly, it's just listening, knowing there's someone to listen.

Tark: Do you ever...I mean, can you talk with other kids? (*He is nervous and agitated.*)

Dianne: Sure. If someone's having a problem, we're glad to listen. That's the whole purpose. (*She turns and looks at* **Tark**.) What is it, Tark? Is something bothering you?

Tark: It's something I never told anyone. Except my parents. (*He hesitates.*) This is hard, Dianne. It's really a big risk for me. It's something about me.

Dianne: Whatever it is, Tark, it's OK. (*She smiles.*) Believe me, you can trust me. And I won't tell anyone else. Not if you don't want me to.

Tark: OK. (*He sighs deeply.*) Dianne, I'm gay. That's it, OK? I'm...I'm gay.

Dianne: And you're afraid to let other people know, is that it?

Tark: I told my parents, so I must be crazy, right? I didn't have to tell them, did I? But I couldn't live with it anymore by myself. I thought I'd explode or something. Keeping it all inside, not knowing what to do.

Dianne: You've known about yourself for a long time?

Tark: Since I was a little kid. (*He swallows hard.*) I don't know if you want to listen to this.

Dianne: Go on.

Tark: First, it was people like my teachers. Men teachers. Or—this is really weird—guys I'd see in the movies or on T.V. I didn't understand what I felt, except that I wanted to be around them. I wanted to be friends with them.

Dianne: You wanted to be friends?

Tark: It was like a curse. I couldn't think of anything else. I started in elementary school. Maybe even first or second grade. I'd want so much to be with these men. It wasn't sex—I was too young for that. And I guess, maybe, I thought everyone had feelings like I did. It was only later I realized they didn't.

Dianne: What do you mean?

Tark: All the laughing, the jokes. About, you know, "queers" and "homos."

Dianne: It must have really hurt.

Tark: I felt so dishonest, so guilty, because I went along with all of it. I put down kids like that too. I made fun of them. Kids who were effeminate...or whatever.

Dianne: I can sympathize. Sometimes, it's easier to go along with the crowd, even though it destroys a little bit of yourself.

Tark: I appreciate your listening to me. Maybe you do understand. Anyhow, I decided to tell my parents how I felt.

Dianne: You want to tell me what happened?

Tark: Yeah. I told Mom first. She was in the kitchen, cooking dinner. It probably wasn't the best time. But there isn't any "best time," I guess. So I just blurted it out. "I'm gay, Mom," I said. At first she didn't believe me. It was like it was some kind of bad joke. Like she was waiting for the punch line.

Dianne: I can see you were taking an awfully big risk.

Tark: And then she stared at me and said I was just imagining it. And she said she wanted me to see a shrink. I turned and ran up to my room.

Dianne: Did you talk to her later?

Tark: I tried. She kept telling me I didn't know what I was saying, that people like that were perverts. I don't remember all that she said.

Dianne: What about your dad?

Tark: He and I always had a good relationship. At least, I thought we did. I was never as good at some things as he thought I should be. And I felt I was a kind of disappointment to him.

Dianne: What do you mean?

Tark: Oh, you know. He's successful at everything he does. He's a good salesman, a good bowler. He got the best grades in school. I don't care about those things. It sounds kind of dumb, but what I care about is people, I guess. They're most important. (*He closes his eyes for a moment and bites his lip.*) He called me all kinds of things. He threatened to kick me out. We were in the living room. Mom heard us arguing and came in. "Frank," she said. "Stop. He's our son." "Some son," he told her. "The kid's a little faggot. Didn't you hear what he said?"

Dianne: That's really rough.

Tark: I grabbed my jacket and left. I walked for hours.

Dianne: But you finally went home?

Tark: Yeah. Mom met me at the door and started telling me all this stuff about AIDS, you know? On and on and on. I tried to tell her I knew all that stuff. I know what to do. She said I'd just have to "control my urges." She was putting me on my honor, she and Dad. But if they knew I was...I was with someone...

Dianne: It's OK, Tark.

Tark: ...they said they'd kick me out.

Dianne: It's sounds to me like you have some pretty heavy things happening.

Tark: That's putting it mildly.

Questions for Discussion

1. Dianne is being a peer counselor as she listens to Tark's story. Discuss the importance of having a person such as Dianne be available for Tark.

2. What are some of Dianne's statements or questions that reveal her to be a caring and nonjudgmental person?

3. What are some strategies that Tark could use to communicate better with his parents?

4. If you were the peer counselor talking to Tark, what are some things you might do to help him?

5. Discuss the feelings of Tark's parents. What are their options?

Having a Gay Parent

*The action takes place in the living room of Debbie's home. Present are **Kevin**, **Jim** and several other teenagers. It is a meeting of an organization for children of gay parents.*

Debbie: It was a real shock to find out about my father. I mean, I'd heard about people like that, but I never thought my dad was that way.

Jim: How did you find out?

Debbie: It all started with a silly argument. Mom had been dead a little over a year, and I guess I was kind of angry at the whole world—Dad, especially. I had to take my anger out on someone.

Kevin: I was mad at my dad too. My mom died when I was twelve. And Dad was hardly ever there.

Debbie: Well, my dad's here. He's a commercial artist and works at home. I sometimes wished it'd been him instead of Mom who died.

Kevin: I had the same thought.

Debbie: A lot of kids must feel that way when a parent dies. What about you, Jim?

Jim: Oh, my mom didn't die. She and Dad got divorced.

Kevin: But don't you live with your dad?

Jim: Yes.

Kevin: I just assumed —

Jim: That I'd want to stay with Mom.

Kevin: Yeah. I don't want to be nosy, but...

Jim: Dad's a lot more fun to be with. So are his friends. And they're a heck of a lot more accepting. I guess what I'm saying is that they treat me as an equal. I love Mom, and I want her to be a part of my life, but with her I'm kind of, well, demoted in rank.

Debbie: You mean it's a parent-child thing there. But when you're with your father, you're an equal.

Jim: Right.

Debbie: Why do you think that is?

Jim: I don't know. Maybe it's because so many gays have suffered rejection that they're a little more tolerant. Everyone can kind of do or be what he wants. I don't mean I have complete freedom. But if I'm out on a date, and the movie or whatever runs a little long, I don't have to worry about being grounded or anything. I call Dad and let him know. It's no big deal.

Kevin: I kind of wish it was a big deal with me. I'm really on my own. I have been for a long time. It's like...like Dad doesn't know I exist.

Sally: You guys all have a gay father. It's my mother who's gay. A lesbian.

Debbie: How do you feel about that?

Sally: It took getting used to. Especially when Ruth moved in.

Kevin: Ruth?

Sally: Mom's..."wife," as she calls her.

Jim: It was rough, huh?

Sally: I was worried about what my friends would think. I was only fourteen.

Debbie: Did you know at the time that your mother was gay?

Sally: Maybe I thought it was a reaction.

Jim: I don't follow.

Sally: She used to give these talks. About being a battered women. About my father

Jim: Your father beat her?

Sally: I hardly remember all that. We left when I was seven.

Debbie: How do you feel about things now? Your mother and Ruth?

Sally: I've accepted it, I guess. It took awhile. But anyway, Debbie, you were telling us about what happened with your father.

Debbie: What was I saying? I know. All this happened about a year and a half ago. Dad was in his studio, working. It's really the enclosed porch. You have to pass through it to get inside. I'd just gotten off the school bus when Dad asked if I'd mind fixing dinner.

Jim: Was that your job?

Debbie: Not really. He was working and didn't want to stop. But, darn it, he was always working.

Jim: Maybe he missed your mom, and that was how he dealt with it.

Debbie: Looking back, I suppose that's true. At first, when I found out about him, I thought he must have been fooling us all along. That he didn't love any of us, especially Mom. How could he?

Kevin: You said you thought this at first. Did you change your mind?

Debbie: I know he loved Mom. Her dying was hard on all of us, but especially on Dad. Because of his job, he has to be alone so much. My brother and sister and I have school. At least we get out of the house.

Jim: I think my dad loved...loves my mom too. But in a different kind of way. They're still good friends. I suppose he just didn't want to go on living a lie.

Debbie: When Dad asked me to get dinner, I acted like a jerk. I told him I had a lot of homework, but, *if he insisted,* I'd do what he wanted.

Kevin: What did he say?

Debbie: Not much of anything, even when I accused him of always asking me instead of my sister or brother. I could tell that made him mad, but he didn't answer. He just stood up and walked to the door. That made me mad too.

(She looks down at her hands.) It's kind of embarrassing what happened.

Jim: You don't need to be embarrassed, Deb. We've all done things we don't like to talk about.

Debbie: (*Smiles at* **Jim.**) I guess I missed Mom more than I knew. It's a terrible thing not to have her around. Not to have her see you going to your first big dance. Her not being there to take for a ride when you get your driver's license.

Kevin *nods.*

Debbie: I started screaming this stuff at Dad about how he didn't care about us, and how the whole family had fallen apart since Mom died. He walked outside and around the house and out through the back. I yelled at him that I said I'd fix dinner, and why was he just walking off. (**Debbie** *swallows hard.*)

Jim: It's OK, Deb. Both of you were hurting, and you had to do something about it.

Debbie: Dad went on down the hill to the railroad track and started walking toward town. I ran after him, screaming. He didn't pay any attention, and I started to cry. I guess I got a little hysterical.

Kevin: Did he ever answer you?

Debbie: He answered, all right.

Jim: What did he say?

Debbie: It's not so much what he said. It's what I said then. I was mad and was trying to make him listen. I yelled, "Do you know what your trouble is?" He still didn't pay any attention. And that made me angrier. "I'll tell you," I said. "You need to get married again."

Jim: Wow. What did he say?

Debbie: He turned around and just stood there. "What did you say?" he finally asked. (*She breathes deeply.*) I told him he didn't care about anything or anybody. That he was grouchy all the time, and that I was tired of it. And then I asked him why didn't he go find a wife.

Kevin: I'd hate to think what would happen if I'd ever say something like that to my dad.

Debbie: I could tell he was angry, angrier than I'd ever seen him. But when he spoke, his voice was quiet. "Maybe I'm gay," he said. I couldn't believe it. "Are you?" I said.

Jim: It must have been awful. You didn't suspect?

Debbie: No. I know he never cheated on Mom. I know that for sure. They did everything together. There'd have been no opportunity. After I asked him if he were gay and he said, "Yes," it was like my whole world came apart. I had nothing to hold onto.

Jim: What did you do?

Debbie: I don't remember. I know I talked to my sister. I couldn't keep it all to myself. I hated him so much at first. It was like he was betraying all of us, especially Mom. I'd lived with him all my life, but I felt I didn't know him.

Kevin: Me too, Debbie. But I never got over the feeling.

Jim: You still feel that way?

Kevin: With reason. I suspected long before Mom died that dad was having sex with men. I was pretty young, but I knew the score. Looking back, I guess I can understand a little. I mean Mom was sick for a long time before she died. And I suppose Dad needed someone...

Jim: But why did it have to be other men, right?

Kevin: I did feel that way. And then, after Mom died, I was really pretty lonely. I tried to talk to him once, to tell him that it was OK if he was gay. The guy who owned the store on the corner—he was gay. Everybody knew that. The other kids made fun of him sometimes, but I never did.

Debbie: So, what happened?

Kevin: It seemed like Dad was really paying attention to what I said. He put his arm around me, and he had tears in his eyes. But later, things were just the same as before.

Jim: You know what, Kev? I think it's more than your father's sexual preferences that's at the base of all this.

Kevin: Oh?

Jim: Maybe he's just the kind of man who can't relate well to kids.

Kevin: Maybe. He and I never did get along. I still live at the house, but I have my own separate little apartment there. I buy my clothes and food and everything with money Mom left me. Dad owns the house and pays the utilities, but otherwise, it's like I'm on my own.

Debbie: You never tried to talk after that one time?

Kevin: I didn't see any point.

Questions for Discussion

1. How do you think Debbie felt when she found out about her father?

2. Compare Debbie's situation to Kevin's. Which one do you think is more fortunate? Why?

3. What reason does Jim give for his father's being more accepting than his mother?

4. If you were a peer counselor and Debbie was assigned to you, what would be your options if you felt a strong bias against homosexuals?

5. Jim says maybe Kevin's dad is just the kind of man who can't relate well to kids. What characteristics do you see in people who do not relate well to kids?

6. Should Debbie's father have told her that he was gay? Why or why not?

7. What are some of the things Kevin's dad might have wanted to say to his son, but couldn't?

8. As a peer counselor, would you find it easier to counsel Kevin or Debbie? Or would there be no difference?

PEER COUNSELING

Personality Clash

The action takes place in a high school
peer counseling class.

Jane: I'm counseling this girl who's new in school, and I really need some help from the class.

Tom: What's the problem, Jane?

Jane: Cindy's having a hard time adjusting. And frankly, I'm getting impatient with her.

Melissa: Should you refer her to another peer counselor?

Jane: Maybe. That's why I want to talk to the class. I need your input.

Tom: Can you tell us more?

Jane: Cindy approached me one day when I was wearing my peer counseling shirt. She said she'd been told peer counselors were available for those who needed them. I told her that was right, and we agreed to meet after school.

Melissa: I bet she didn't show up.

Jane: Oh, yes, she did. That's not one of her problems. She *always* shows up.

Tom: (*Jokingly.*) Sounds like you sometimes wish she wouldn't.

Jane: That's how I feel about half the time.

Melissa: That bad, huh?

Jane: I don't want to make this bigger than it is. Cindy's not a bad person. She just gets on my nerves.

Tom: Maybe you'd better explain.

Jane: I know we're supposed to be accepting and tolerant. I've tried. But Cindy has certain habits that drive me up a wall.

Melissa: Personal habits, you mean?

Jane: She whines all the time, worse than any two year old. She's a very negative person.

Tom: Tell us what you've already tried.

Jane: When I first started seeing her—about two months ago—I just let her talk. She seemed lonely, and I thought she needed someone to listen.

Tom: I take it that didn't help.

Jane: It seemed like it did at first, but there was no carry-over. Each time I met with her, I found her to be as miserable as she'd ever been.

Melissa: Could you tell us a little more about her?

Jane: She moved here from a small town in Utah. She tells me she had a lot of friends and was involved in lots of school activities.

Melissa: Are you implying you haven't been able to get her involved in activities here?

Jane: Right. And that's what I don't understand. If she was involved in her last school, why not here?

Tom: You've told her about all the clubs on campus and how easy it is to join?

Jane: I've gone even further than that. I've taken her to meetings and introduced her to the members.

Tom: What happened? Didn't she want to join?

Jane: She always had some excuse.

Tom: Like what?

Jane: She didn't feel she fit in, or the clubs weren't like those at her old school. I've heard what it was like at her old school so many times, I could scream. I felt like asking her why she didn't go back where she came from.

Melissa: I can see how it might be hard for someone from a small school like that to move to a large one. There'd be a lot of differences.

Jane: I agree, Melissa. I've told myself a thousand times that it must be hard for her now, that she just needs friends and time to adjust. But she isn't making any friends, and she certainly isn't any better adjusted than she was two months ago. I guess what I'm saying is that I've really failed in trying to help her.

Tom: How about changing that a little? Why not just believe you haven't succeeded yet?

Jane: But that's the problem. I don't think I will succeed. I've let the whining get to me. I'm tired of listening to her tell me how unfriendly everyone here is, how stuck-up they are, how involved they are in their own cliques. I know for a fact that several people I've introduced her to have gone out of their way to be nice to her. But she doesn't accept them. And so they stop trying.

Questions for Discussion

1. What are the alternatives Jane could use in trying to help her counselee?

2. List some of the challenges in moving from a small school to a large one. List ways to meet these challenges.

3. Do you think Cindy was involved in activities in her previous school, as she says she was? Why do you think she has excuses each time for not getting involved at her new school?

4. Do you feel Jane should refer Cindy to another peer counselor? Why or why not?

5. List ways of improving a negative attitude.

What Do I Do Now?

The action takes place in a peer counseling class.

Faye: I knew something like this would happen. I just didn't think it would be with my very first counselee. Now, I'm even having doubts about being a peer counselor.

Wendy: What is it?

Faye: Today I wore my peer counseling shirt for the first time, like everyone else. I didn't think anyone would come up to me — not the first day.

Bob: No one's come up to me.

Faye: You're lucky.

Wendy: I don't understand. This is why we trained for a whole semester.

Bob: For me it's like opening night of a play. I knew I was ready, but I still had butterflies.

Faye: I know, but this is worse. The person who came up to me wants me to do something I think is wrong.

Wendy: You'd better start at the beginning.

Faye: It was a ninth-grade girl. Thirteen or fourteen. She came up to me after P.E. She saw my shirt and wanted to know if I talked to people with problems.

Bob: Did you know her?

Faye: Not really. Our gym lockers are close together, and I talk to her when I see her, but that's all. Anyhow, she asked if we could meet later. I guess I was a little flattered.

Wendy: What made you change your mind?

Faye: She told me she's pregnant and wants an abortion. It was not what I expected at all. I thought maybe she needed tutoring or something, or was having a problem at home. I was really shocked.

Wendy: Did she know how you felt?

Faye: Yes. I'm afraid I didn't handle things very well.

Bob: What did you do?

Faye: I thought about what we learned in class—about not having to help someone if it goes against our own values.

Bob: That's true.

Faye: I told her I didn't believe in abortion and couldn't help her. But that I'd be glad to refer her to another peer counselor.

Bob: Sounds like you did what you should. What's the problem?

Faye: She started crying. She said I was judging her, and she thought peer counselors weren't supposed to do that. I tried to tell her I wasn't judging her as a person, just that I feel differently about abortion than she does.

Wendy: Did she understand?

Faye: I don't think so. In fact, I don't think she understands the whole thing. She's just an innocent kid who got caught the first time she had sex with her boyfriend.

Wendy: How did you leave things?

Faye: We talked about options, things I don't think she had even thought about.

Bob: Has she talked to her parents?

Faye: No. She's afraid to tell them. I tried to explain that it might help, depending on the type of people they are.

Wendy: Are you going to meet her again?

Faye: Yes, and I don't know what to do about it. She begged me not to refer her to someone else. I guess she feels comfortable with me or something. She's desperate to have someone to talk to.

Bob: That doesn't solve the situation?

Faye: No, it doesn't. If she still wants an abortion, I'll have to refer her to someone else.

Questions for Discussion

1. Discuss Faye's role as a peer counselor. List the things you feel were her strengths and weaknesses, if any.

2. Faye brings her problem back to the peer counseling class for discussion and input. Discuss the value of doing this.

3. Why is it important to refer someone to another peer counselor if the counselee's situation creates problems for the counselor?

4. Does Faye give advice when she encourages the counselee to tell her parents? Why or why not?

5. Do most peer counselors feel some anxiety when they begin to have contact with counselees? If so, how can they deal with it?

Brother with a Bad Reputation

The action occurs as **Susan** *and* **Bill** *are walking home from school.*

Susan: What's wrong, Bill? You haven't said two words since we left school.

Bill: Nothing.

Susan: Don't give me that. We've been dating too long for you to try to fool me.

Bill: Gene's coming home tonight.

Susan: Your brother?

Bill: The one and only.

Susan: I thought he'd be in Florida permanently.

Bill: So did I.

Susan: Wow! I can see why you're depressed.

Bill *nods.*

Susan: Will he be here long?

Bill: I'm afraid he'll be with Dad and me permanently. Dad said Mom couldn't handle him, so she's sending him back.

Susan: No one can handle Gene, can they? (*Pause.*) I'm sorry. He's your brother, and I shouldn't talk like that. It's just that he's already been in so much trouble.

Bill: Don't apologize. He's my brother, but I sometimes feel we aren't related at all.

Susan: You couldn't be more different, that's for sure. You do everything right. He does everything wrong.

Bill: Let's just say we have different value systems. He doesn't respect anyone, including himself. And he's out to get whatever he can, no matter what.

Susan: I don't see how you two could have been raised in the same house.

Bill: My parents could never figure it out. They always treated Gene and me the same. They never played favorites. But he's always caused trouble.

Susan: I remember your telling me your mom almost had a nervous breakdown. When Gene stole the motorcycle.

Bill: Yeah. (*Looks toward* **Susan**.) I think that was the beginning of the end for her and Dad. I don't think they'd be divorced if it wasn't for all the trouble Gene got into. It put too much pressure on the whole family.

Susan: It doesn't seem fair, does it? I mean, that he's caused so much trouble for everyone.

Bill: What's not fair is that he's coming back to disrupt my life again. Mine and Dad's.

Susan: What can you do about it? Anything?

Bill: (*Shrugs.*) Not really, I guess. See, when Gene's back, everyone talks about "that wild Carson kid." A lot of people don't bother to ask which one. Because he's my brother, people think I'm that way too.

Susan: (*Laughing.*) I still remember how my father came unglued when he found out you and I were going to the prom. That was before he met you.

Bill: Yeah, he hadn't met Gene either, but he'd certainly heard about him.

Susan: I know this sounds crazy. But since you can't stop Gene from coming here, do you think there's any way you can help him?

Bill: You mean, because I'm a peer counselor?

Susan *nods.*

Bill: (*Sighs.*) I've thought about that a lot. How can I justify being a peer counselor if I don't try to help my own brother?

Susan: But you have tried in the past. Your entire family tried — over and over again.

Bill: Yeah, I know. But nothing did any good, so far as I could see. I got fed up with it.

Susan: And a little angry?

Bill: (*Laughs without humor.*) Yes, and a little angry. I was so relieved when he moved. And you know, that makes me feel guilty, too. That I'm not a very concerned person.

Susan: I understand. You're so good at peer counseling. You have a reputation as one of the best on campus. And where your brother's concerned, that puts you in a real bind, right?

Bill: What do you mean?

Susan: I mean, that it's hard to balance your reputation as a peer counselor against the fact that you can't help your own brother.

Bill: It's worse than that. I don't even want to help him. I just want him to go away.

Susan: Don't you think that's normal after what you've been through?

Bill: Maybe, but I still feel guilty. I'm supposed to be a caring, concerned person. But I'm not.

Susan: That's not true. You are a caring person.

Bill: But don't you see? If I'm not caring with my brother, then I'm really not at all. I'm a hypocrite, and my reputation's a joke.

Susan: I think you're being much too hard on yourself. Remember, it's Gene who has the problems, not you.

Bill: Now we both do. The only difference is, Gene doesn't worry about his, and I do.

Susan: Why don't you talk to the peer counseling teacher?

Bill: I guess I should. I don't even know if I should continue as a peer counselor.

Questions for Discussion

1. Discuss ways that Bill might help his brother.

2. Does it make Bill an uncaring person if he continues to feel the same way about his brother? Why or why not?

3. If Bill decides not to try to help his brother, should he remain a peer counselor? Why or why not?

4. Besides "anger," what are some words to describe Bill?

5. What other alternatives does Bill have besides living with his father and brother?

6. Discuss the word "reputation." What factors go into making one's reputation?

7. How important is it to have a good reputation? Why?

8. What are the drawbacks of a peer counselor trying to help a member of his or her own family?

PREGNANCY

Teen Pregnancy and Abortion

*The action takes place in Julie's home. The scene begins when **Julie** enters her father's study, where he is busy going over papers related to his job. **Julie** is the younger of two daughters. Her mother died years before.*

Julie: (*Hesitating in the study doorway.*) Dad?

Dad: (*Looking up, irritated at the interruption.*) What is it?

Julie: If it's not a good time, I'll come back.

Dad: Is something wrong?

Julie: There's something I have to talk to you about. I've been putting it off. But I just can't deal with it anymore.

Dad: This sounds pretty serious.

Julie: (*She comes around the desk and sits in an extra chair near **Dad**.*) Yeah. (*She looks into his eyes.*) I don't want you to hate me.

Dad: Why would I hate you?

Julie: You don't know what I've done.

Dad: Look, Julie, before we go any further, I want to tell you something. OK?

Julie: OK.

Dad: (*Smiles, a little sadly.*) You're my daughter, and I love you. There's nothing you could do that I can think of that would make me hate you. I love you.

Julie: (*Crying.*) Oh, Daddy, I don't know how I can tell you.

Dad: I think I have a pretty good idea.

Julie: Did Sue tell you? She's the only one who knew. She didn't talk to you, did she?

Dad: No, nobody talked to me.

Julie: Then how do you know?

Dad: I've been a parent for a long time, Julie.

Julie: You won't get mad, will you?

Dad: I honestly don't know. I may.

Julie: (*She stands up, walks to the door and turns back.*) Daddy, I was pregnant.

Dad: Was? You're not anymore.

Julie: I didn't know what to do. Remember what you said a long time ago? That you couldn't raise any more kids. You were getting too old.

Dad: I remember.

Julie: What was I going to do? Oh, Daddy, I went to a clinic.

Dad: And you had an abortion, is that it?

Julie: I was so scared. I didn't want to have the baby. I know that after Mom died, it was rough on you. Having to take care of us all alone. And —

Dad: And I jokingly told you and your sister that if either of you became pregnant, I wouldn't have the kid in my house. (*Shakes his head.*) It was a joke, Julie. A bad joke.

Julie: I thought you meant it. You sounded like you meant it.

Dad: Maybe I did. I don't know. But that doesn't matter now, does it?

Julie: Do you know what Sue called me? A baby killer. A murderer.

Dad: I can't believe she'd do that.

Julie: She did.

Dad: How do you feel about it? About the abortion, I mean.

Julie: I just want to know how you feel.

Dad: That isn't important right now. How you feel is.

Julie: I can tell you're mad.

Dad: I suppose. Can you blame me? You felt you couldn't come to me. You couldn't trust me. Maybe that means I've failed. Maybe I'm mad at me as well as at you.

Julie: What about the abortion, Daddy? What do you think about that?

Dad: It'll take some getting used to. There's no use pretending it won't. (*He runs a hand through his hair.*) I've made no secret of how I've always felt. Except for some very specific reasons, I've always been against abortion. But now my feelings are all mixed up. I can't figure out all the things I'm feeling.

Julie: Will you forgive me?

Dad: I love you, Julie. Like I said, I'll always love you. Isn't that enough for now?

Questions for Discussion

1. Why do you think Julie didn't tell her dad she was pregnant?

2. Why do you think she told him after she had the abortion?

3. Did her dad respond in an effective way? What do you think he was feeling, but not saying?

4. Compare Julie's feelings to those of her father. What are some other feelings, besides *love* and *guilt*, that could apply to both of them?

5. Julie's father didn't ask about the father of the baby. Why do you think he didn't?

Teenage Father

The action occurs on the sidewalk in front of the school where **Russ** *and* **Jeff** *are talking.*

Jeff: It's not at all like I thought it would be.

Russ: In what way?

Jeff: I love Tammy and Brad, but it's rough.

Russ: I'll bet.

Jeff: There's no money for anything extra. We're living upstairs at her parents' house. It's supposed to be private, but it's not. They can hear everything that goes on, and we can hear them. I never knew as much about my own folks.

Russ: At least you can stay in school. That helps, doesn't it?

Jeff: I had all kinds of plans. I wanted to be an engineer. That was the most important thing in my life. So what am I doing? Working in a shop, running a dumb machine. I hardly ever see Tammy and Brad. I'm home for an hour

242

after school, and then I go to work. A full shift. By the time I get home, after one A.M., they're long since asleep.

Russ: What about weekends?

Jeff: I'm so tired I can hardly do anything. I try to get my schoolwork done, but I don't have the energy. Most of the teachers understand. They've tried to work things out, so most of my assignments are due on Monday. Still, it's no life. And I don't even know why I'm bothering to finish.

Russ: I'm glad I'm not in your shoes.

Jeff: Sometimes I want to run as far away as I can. Escape the responsibility. But I can't. I couldn't do that to Brad. Or to Tammy.

Russ: Is she still in school?

Jeff: Part-time. Evenings, at a special school. It'll take her forever to finish.

Russ: Hey, listen, if there's anything I can do...

Jeff: Yeah. (*He looks into Russ' eyes.*) You know what I miss most?

Russ: What?

Jeff: Seeing old friends. We can never go anywhere, do anything. I only see you because we're in the same class. And this is the first time we've had a chance to talk, only because I'm waiting for Tammy's mom to pick me up. She's late, which means I'll have to leave right away for work.

Russ: Do you guys ever get a babysitter?

Jeff: Are you kidding? Even if we did, where could we go? What could we do? Tammy's mom watches Brad while she's in school. But that's it.

Russ: I have an idea. See what you think. We take turns watching Brad. Some of the gang. Your friends and Tammy's. Then every weekend, say every Saturday or Sunday night, the rest of us get together with you and Tammy and do something. Something that doesn't cost money.

Jeff: Like what?

Russ: I don't know. Hang out, maybe. Go to the park. Whatever. We'll work it out.

Jeff: Hey, man, you know, I really appreciate this. But it doesn't solve anything. Not the basic problems. I mean, it'll give us a change...

Russ: Parties, Jeff. We could take turns having parties. Soft drinks and chips.

Jeff: What I started to say was that I'd like you to go on and try, if you want to. But I'll still have to work my butt off. Tammy and I can't really be one of the crowd anymore.

Russ: How's Tammy taking all this?

Jeff: It's rough on her, too. She doesn't complain. And I feel so sorry. So inadequate. I mean, a guy's supposed to provide for his family. Give them a good life. Ah, Russ, what did I get myself into? (*There's the sound of a car pulling over and stopping.*) Oh, there's my mother-in-law. I've got to get going.

Russ: Yeah, Jeff. OK, buddy. You take care, you hear?

Questions for Discussions

1. What qualities do you admire most in Jeff? What do you admire the least?

2. What could Jeff have done differently to avoid his situation?

3. What can Tammy do to help the situation?

4. What do you think are the chances of Jeff and Tammy ever having a "normal" life?

5. Is Russ' suggestion for helping Jeff and Tammy realistic? Why? Why not?

Dealing with Pregnancy

The action takes place on the sidewalk in front of Geoff's house. He and **Trudy** *are talking.*

Trudy: Dad and Mom will kill me. I know they'll just kill me.

Geoff: What are you going to do?

Trudy: What am *I* going to do? What about you? What about us?

Geoff: That's what I meant.

Trudy: Did you?

Geoff: Trudy, I love you. I'm so sorry this had to happen.

Trudy: Yeah. But *sorry* doesn't help. I don't know what's going to help. If only we'd waited...

Geoff: (*Putting his arm around her shoulder.*) It's done, Trudy. It's over and done with.

Trudy: (*Pulling away.*) No, Geoff, it's not over. It's only just starting.

Geoff: What about, you know...a clinic or something?

Trudy: Abortion? Geoff—

Geoff: I can't get married. What kind of life would that be?

Trudy: It's easier for you. You can hide what happened, and no one would even know. Your parents would never know.

Geoff: (*Sighing.*) Right. That's right, Trudy. I can just walk away and forget it happened. Is that what you're saying?

Trudy: You could.

Geoff: I don't think so. How could I live with myself?

The lights fade to black.

Scene ii

The action occurs in Geoff's home.
He enters the living room, where his mother and father
are watching TV.

Geoff: Mom, Dad, I've got to talk to you.

Dad: What is it, Geoff? It sounds serious.

Geoff: I don't know how to tell you. It's about— (*He breaks off and shakes his head.*) I... I...

Mom: Whatever it is, Geoff, we'll try to help.

Geoff: You're going to hate me. I know you will.

Dad: (*Rising and turning off the TV set.*) I doubt that very much. (*He tries to smile.*)

Mom: What happened? Did something happen?

Geoff: Trudy thought I might walk away, but I can't. I really can't. (*Taking a deep breath.*) It's about Trudy and me. I know you won't want to hear this, but she and I...

As he continues to talk, the lights fade to black, cutting off his voice.

Scene iii

The lights come up in the home of Trudy's Aunt **Gloria.** **Trudy** *and* **Gloria** *are sitting at the kitchen table.*

Trudy: Anyhow, I had to talk to you. I had to talk to someone.

Gloria: I'm flattered that you trust me that much.

Trudy: Thanks. (*Sighs.*) Oh, Aunt Gloria, what am I going to do?

Gloria: (*Reaching across the table to take Trudy's hand.*) What is it, honey? You know I'll help, if I can.

Trudy: (*Crying.*) Aunt Glory, I'm pregnant.

Gloria: Oh, honey, I'm so sorry. Are you sure?

Trudy *nods.*

Gloria: How far along?

Trudy: A couple of months.

Gloria: And you don't know what to do?

Trudy: What about Mom and Dad? How are they going to react?

Gloria: They're pretty nice people. (*Lightly.*) I wouldn't have a sister and brother-in-law who weren't, you know.

Trudy: How can I tell them?

Gloria: We'll try to work something out. I'll be there, if you like. OK?

Trudy: Thanks. I'll have to think about it. How I'm going to do it, you know?

Questions for Discussion

1. What choices does Trudy have?

2. What choices does Geoff have?

3. Why do you think it is easier for Geoff to talk to his parents than for Judy to talk to hers? Or is it?

4. Why do you think Judy goes to her aunt instead of to her mother?

5. Trudy says, "If only we'd waited." What are some of the positive aspects of waiting? List some of the reasons why teenagers don't wait.

6. List some of the ways this pregnancy will affect Geoff's and Trudy's lives.

7. Whose life do you think will be most affected?

RACE

Biracial Teenager

The action takes place around the dining table of the Patterson home.

Gerry: How y'all doin' tonight, Toni?

Toni: Gerry, why do you have to do that?

Mom: What's this all about, Gerry?

Gerry: Nothing, Mom. It's just that Toni's starting to hang around with all the black kids. She tries to talk like them and everything.

Mom: Why does that bother you?

Gerry: Come on, Mom. She doesn't have to talk like that.

Toni: You don't have to make fun of me. I hate it when you make fun of me. You're half black, too.

Gerry: Yeah, half. And half white.

Toni: Are you ashamed of the black part?

Gerry: No, I'm not ashamed. It's just that you're trying to pretend. You're identifying with black kids. You have hardly any white friends.

Toni: What about you? Do you have any black friends?

Gerry: It's none of your business, but, yeah, I have black friends.

Toni: Name two.

Mom: All right, that's enough. I don't want the dinner table turned into a battleground. I don't know why it's such a big deal, anyway. Your dad and I have always tried to teach you that people are people. That's the only important thing.

Toni: Sure, Mom. But you and Dad are white.

Dad: What do you mean by that, Toni?

Toni: There's half of me, Dad. Half of me that I don't know anything about.

Dad: (*Sighs.*) I realize that, honey. But I don't know what to do about it. Your mom and I are what we are. As your adoptive parents, we've lived a certain way, come from a certain cultural background. With your biological parents it was different. One was black, one was white. I know it must be hard.

Toni: (*Looking at Gerry.*) At least I don't try to deny half of me, like some people I know.

Gerry: Come on, Sis, I don't deny it.

Toni: Yes, you do. You don't look black. If anything, people think you look Hispanic.

Gerry: And I'm supposed to feel guilty about that?

Toni: No...yes...well, maybe you are. I'll bet your girlfriend Katie doesn't even know, does she?

Gerry: So what if she doesn't?

Toni: Why don't you tell her? The boys I date know about me.

Gerry: Of course, they do. They have eyes.

Toni: I'll bet you've never told anyone.

Gerry: Look, Toni, you just worry about yourself.

Toni: Not when you make fun of me.

Gerry: Do you remember before we moved here? That school we went to, out in the country?

Toni: Of course, I remember.

Gerry: OK, then. Do you remember when those boys started to call you names?

Toni: I remember.

Gerry: Who was it that got a bloody nose trying to make them take it back?

Toni: (*Sighs.*) You still don't need to make fun of me, Gerry.

Gerry: I'm sorry, OK?

Toni: You know what? It's not easy. I'm not black and I'm not white. I talk white and look black. Kids call me zebra. Or chocolate marshmallow. Or Oreo cookie.

Dad: We love you, Ton. Your mom and I love you. Keep that in mind. I know it won't help all the hurt, but it's something.

Gerry: Remember that time we were in the store, and those two people came up, sounding really angry, and called us names?

Toni: I remember. All the other things, too. The name calling. The stares, the dirty looks. It's not so bad since we moved, I guess.

Gerry: You know, Toni, you're right. I *have* denied one half of me, pretended it wasn't there.

Toni: Me too, I guess. I wish it didn't have to be that way.

Questions for Discussion

1. Compare Gerry's and Toni's feelings about being biracial. How are the feelings similar? How are they different?

2. What cultural problems may arise when both the parents are of one race and the children are of another race or are of mixed races?

3. Why do you think Gerry didn't tell his girlfriend he was half black?

4. List some ways you can help people to deal with their prejudices.

5. Ask members of the class to share how they feel when they find themselves in the minority, no matter what color they are.

Interracial Dating

Scene i

The scene is the living room of the Foster home.

Heidi: He's going to be here in a few minutes. Please, Daddy —

Dad: I don't understand you. Your grandmother and grand-father would turn over in their graves —

Heidi: What's so bad about it?

Dad: I shouldn't have to explain it. In my time, nobody like your so-called "friend" would even *talk* to someone like you.

Heidi: What do you mean, Dad, "someone like me?"

Dad: You know perfectly well what I mean.

Heidi: No, I don't. You'll have to tell me.

Dad: Shape up, young lady. It's only for your mother's sake that I agreed to this. For my part, I think it's disgraceful. No self-respecting girl would want to be seen —

Heidi: With someone like Warren? Oh, come on, Dad, that kind of thinking went out with the dark ages.

Dad: Not for me. I know there are plenty of people who don't agree with me. But God made us separate, and that's how we should stay.

Heidi: You mean you believe in segregation? Nobody believes in segregation anymore.

Dad: As far as dating and marriage, I do. No good can come of racial mixing.

Heidi: Well, I think you're wrong. Some of the best-known people are of mixed race. Actors and writers and singers.

Dad: Exceptions, not the rule.

Heidi: I don't understand you.

Dad: Don't you have any racial pride?

Heidi: Yes, I have racial pride. I'm proud of the accomplishments of the *human* race.

Dad: Don't get uppity with me, young lady.

Heidi: For heaven's sake, Daddy!

Dad: Look what white people did to us, Heidi. Kidnaped us, kept us ignorant and in chains. Treated us like cattle, and the women like prostitutes.

There is a knock at the door. **Dad** *storms upstairs as* **Heidi** *goes to let* **Warren** *in. Blackout.*

Scene ii

As the lights come up, we see that **Heidi** *and* **Warren**
have gone dancing. Music plays in the background.
They sit at a small table with a racially mixed group of
other young people.

Warren: How about a Coke, Heidi?

Heidi: Great.

Warren: Be back in a sec. (*He rises and exits.*)

Heidi: (*To* **Mimi**, *who is obviously a close friend.*) I couldn't believe my father tonight. You know, he objects to my dating Warren. He really objects.

Mimi: On what grounds?

Heidi: Would you believe he told me he doesn't believe in interracial dating or marriage? I realize he grew up in a different time, with the lynchings and all that. But this is the present.

Mimi: My parents don't object — at least, openly. But they're much too polite, you know? Cool and polite.

Mara: Well, you know, maybe they're right. Your parents. You're OK, Heidi. I don't mean to put you down. But what do you want with a white guy anyhow?

Heidi: I can't believe you're saying this. I really can't.

Blackout.

Scene iii

The lights come up immediately
at the concession counter.

Warren: (*To a boy in front of him in line.*) Ryan, how's it going? It's been a long time!

Ryan: Warren. Hey, how you been?

Warren: You know, hanging in there.

Ryan: I saw you with that girl.

Warren: Yeah? What about it?

Ryan: What you do's your own business. Sooner or later, you'll come to your senses.

Warren: Why don't you just say it, Ryan?

Ryan: You of all people, buddy. I thought you had better taste than that.

Warren: I don't like what you're saying. About me or about my date. Especially about Heidi.

Ryan: Heidi, is that her name? Cute little Swiss girl.

Warren: (*Gives* **Ryan** *a shove.*) Just back off, all right?

Questions for Discussion

1. Were you surprised when you found out Heidi's dad is black? By his comments to Heidi, do you think many people would presume he is white?

2. List some problems interracial couples might have to face. List some solutions to these problems.

3. Heidi says, "No one believes in segregation anymore." Do you think this is a true statement? Give examples to substantiate your answer.

4. What could Warren do to help Ryan be less judgmental of people of other races?

5. Mara says she doesn't mean to put Heidi down. Do you think her comments are a putdown? Why or why not?

RELATIONSHIPS

Feeling Insecure

The action occurs in the living room of the Parsons'
residence. **Sandy** *is talking with her father.*

Sandy: People bother me, Dad. I just want to get away. Do you understand?

Dad: What happened? Did something happen?

Sandy: Some girl said she's going to beat me up. Just because I talked to her boyfriend.

Dad: What?

Sandy: That's all. I can't help it if he talks to me. I answer people who talk to me. And now this girl is all upset. She thinks I want to take away her boyfriend or something.

Dad: I don't understand. She wants to fight you?

Sandy: I hate this city.

Dad: Do you think the girl will really try to hurt you?

Sandy: I don't know. But it's not just that. I can't get along with anyone here. I don't know what's wrong with everybody. All my friends turn against me.

Dad: What do you mean?

Sandy: Every time I tell anyone something, they blab it all over town.

Dad: Sandy, I know you don't want to hear this, but yes, I've noticed you don't get along with your friends. You're very irritable.

Sandy *begins to leave the room.*

Dad: (*Following* **Sandy**.) I didn't mean to accuse you.

Sandy: You don't understand. (*She reaches the door and turns.*) Nobody understands. (*She turns and hurries from the room.*)

Lori: (*Entering.*) What's wrong with Sandy, Dad?

Dad: Maybe she should tell you.

Lori: She's having trouble with her friends again, isn't she?

Dad: (*Sighing deeply.*) Yes. Now some girl wants to beat her up. Do you know anything about it?

Lori: (*Walking past him and sitting on the sofa.*) No. I almost never see her at school. We have a different set of friends.

Dad: (*Crossing to a chair and sitting.*) Don't say anything to Sandy, but she always seems to pick the worst people for friends.

Lori: You know what I think?

Dad: What?

Lori: I think she chooses the worst possible friends and the worst possible boyfriends because she feels she can't get anyone nice to accept her.

Dad: Maybe you're right.

Lori: You have to admit, her choice of boyfriends is the absolute worst. Kids at school come up to me and ask what my sister sees in Vernon. He does drugs, lies to her, runs around with other girls, and she's still with him.

Dad: Your brother called me the other day about something...that I haven't wanted to talk to her about. Maybe I shouldn't mention to you. But I'd like to see if you know anything about it.

Lori: I think I know what you're talking about. About Tom's friend seeing Sandy and Vernon...

Dad: ...breaking into someone's car.

Lori: Yes.

Dad: Do you know if it's true?

Lori: No, I don't.

Dad: I didn't want to confront Sandy. I don't want to sound like I'm accusing her of anything.

Sandy: (*Entering the room.*) What's going on?

Dad: Nothing, why?

Sandy: Were you talking about me? I thought I heard someone laughing.

Dad: Honey, no one was laughing at you.

Sandy: (*Unsure of herself.*) I thought I heard someone.

Dad: I want to ask you something.

Lori: (*Getting up.*) Excuse me. (*She exits.*)

Sandy: What is it?

Dad: Come here and sit down.

> **Sandy** *crosses to the chair.* **Dad** *takes her hand.*

Dad: I heard some very disturbing news.

Sandy: What about?

Dad: About Vernon. That he's on drugs. That he even deals drugs. I know he carries — or used to carry — a beeper.

Sandy: (*Pulling away.*) So what?

Dad: I'm not blaming you for anything. I just want what's best for you.

Sandy: Maybe "what's best" is just getting away. I really can't stand it here anymore. I have to get away.

Dad: (*Sighs.*) Maybe you're right. I used to think you couldn't run away from your problems. I still believe that. But a change can help.

Sandy: I mean it. I hate it here.

Dad: I know.

Sandy: Part of it *is* Vernon. He uses drugs. I don't, Dad. I never have, you've got to believe me. But with Vernon,

265

it's like I'm not in control. It's like I'm under a kind of spell. Whatever he wants, I do.

Dad: You really want to get away?

Sandy: More than anything else.

Dad: Look, Sandy, I'll have to think about it, OK?

Questions for Discussion

1. List the reasons Sandy gives for wanting to get away. Do you think these are her real reasons?

2. Make a chart of characteristics of insecure persons. On the opposite side, write ways to combat each characteristic.

3. Do you think Sandy's dad should allow her to go away? Why or why not?

4. Do you think Sandy needs to see a professional mental health person? Why or why not?

5. Why do you think Lori appears to be well-adjusted to school and friends while Sandy doesn't?

Experiencing Job Harassment

The action takes place in a peer counseling class.

Barney: We were talking yesterday about sexual harassment on the job. But there are other kinds of harassment too. I've been thinking about this a lot, and I've got to do something about it. I can't just let it go on.

Rae: Are you being harassed?

Barney: In a way, yeah.

Rae: What way? Do you want to tell us about it?

Barney: I work at a fast food restaurant, eighteen to twenty hours a week. I've been there for almost six months, and the manager...well, he seems to have it in for me.

Mac: What do you mean?

Barney: I always get the worst jobs. We're supposed to rotate. Like I'll be the fry cook for so long, and then switch to counter, and so on.

Rae: But that's not what happens?

Barney: I've always been really sensitive about my appearance, you know. Short and skinny. The thick glasses. Well, my manager doesn't get beyond the appearance.

Stewart: (*Kidding.*) He doesn't find you the charming, debonair sophisticate you really are.

Barney: Right, Stew. No, what happens, I guess, is that he thinks he can pick on me. I'm little. I look...well, I look like a wimp, right?

Ginny: Aw, Barney, I never thought you did.

Barney: I've learned to live with it. Anyhow, it's not just that the manager gives me the worst jobs. He doesn't treat me right at all.

Ginny: How do you mean?

Barney: Like I'm dirt or something.

Mac: What's this guy like physically?

Barney: A little taller than I am. A little bit heavier. Why?

Mac: Really, just about your size.

Barney: Well, basically.

Mac: Does that tell you anything? The way he looks, I mean.

Barney: You mean he's the wimp?

Mac: What do you think?

Barney: Could be, huh? Like he's picking on me so he can get back at everybody who ever picked on him.

Rae: So what can you do about it?

Barney: Well, I don't want to be fired. It took me awhile to find this job. And I do like it there. I get along fine with everyone else.

Ginny: You seem to be saying that one alternative is to just go on as you are.

Barney: If you look at it that way, yeah.

Ginny: Any other choices?

Barney: I could try to talk to him, I guess. But I don't think it'll work. He always has to be right.

Ginny: What else?

Barney: File a suit, maybe. I think the people I work with would back me up. But I'm a high school kid. I'm sixteen, for gosh sakes. I wouldn't even know how to go about that.

Stewart: Could you talk to someone about it, like a legal aid person?

Barney: Maybe this is all getting blown out of proportion. Maybe I can just put up with it.

Stewart: Would you really want to do that?

Barney: My job's important. My parents aren't rich. So when I want something, it's up to me to get it. What it boils down to, I guess, is that I either keep quiet about it and go on like I am, or I take some action. I know I've got to decide. But it's not an easy decision to make.

Questions for Discussion

1. Discuss how job harassment and physical appearance are sometimes linked together.

2. Do you think Barney's boss is actually harassing him, or does Barney just feel he is?

3. The class talked about some alternatives for Barney. Can you name others?

4. Barney says his boss always has to be right. Discuss some ways to deal with people who always have to be right.

Siblings

Scene i

The action occurs at the Janssen home, where **Mom, Dad, Rich, Patsy** *and* **Ellen** *are eating dinner.*

Rich: You got in trouble today, didn't you, Patsy?

Patsy: What are you talking about, Rich?

Rich: (*To* **Ellen**.) You should have seen her. Everybody was laughing.

Ellen: What happened?

Patsy: I don't think that's anybody's business.

Rich: It was really dumb, Patty.

Patsy: Don't call me Patty. You know I don't like that.

Rich: Why not, Patty?

Dad: That's enough, Rich.

Mom: Why does the dinner table have to be turned into a battleground every night?

Rich: Maybe if you didn't have such a dumb daughter.

Patsy: What is it, Rich? Why do you have to keep it up?

Rich: Hey, I'm just pointing out what happened at school today.

Patsy: I could point some things out too.

Rich: Like what?

Patsy: What time did you get home today, Richard?

Rich: What's that have to do with anything?

Patsy: Maybe we should talk about Mr. Holmes' class. How about it?

Dad: Why can't we eat in peace?

Patsy: Why don't you ask your son? He's the one who started it.

The lights fade to black.

Scene ii

The action occurs in the bedroom in Jane's house. She and **Patsy** *are talking.*

Patsy: Sometimes I just can't stand my brother. Most of the time, in fact.

Jane: (*Surprised.*) Rich?

Patsy: Yeah, Rich.

Jane: I always thought he was a pretty neat guy.

Patsy: If you lived in the same house, maybe you'd feel different. He always has to be picking on someone. Ellen or me. Usually me. He thinks it's funny or something. I think he's pretty immature.

Jane: You really dislike him that much?

Patsy: (*Pause.*) Yes, I think I do. It's gotten worse over the years. (*Shrugs.*) I know when people live together, there are bound to be disagreements, arguments. But does it have to be all the time? He's in high school, not junior high. Why doesn't he act it?

Jane: How do you react to him?

Patsy: What do you mean?

Jane: Have you ever tried to ignore him when he starts in on you?

Patsy: Believe me, Jane, I've tried everything.

Jane: What about your sister?

Patsy: What about her?

Jane: Do you get along? Do she and Richie get along?

Patsy: We usually stay out of each other's way. She and Rich? Well, they're kind of close.

Jane: If it really bothers you, just try to avoid him.

Patsy: You don't understand, Jane. He won't let that happen. (*Sighs.*) I guess it's no big deal. I just wish things were better between us.

Questions for Discussion

1. How is Rich treating his sister?

2. Does Patsy really want him to change his behavior?

3. Why do you think Rich gets along with Ellen and not with Patsy?

4. What do you think Rich could do to improve the situation? Outline the steps.

5. What could Patsy do to improve the situation? Outline the steps.

6. Whom do you feel is right, Patsy or Rich? Or is there a right or wrong in this situation?

7. Should the parents become more involved?

Having No Friends

*The action takes place in the hallway outside a
classroom.* **Todd** *is leaning against the wall, waiting to
go inside the room.* **Walt** *walks up to him.*

Walt: Hi, Todd, what's up?

Todd: (*Uncomfortable.*) Nothing.

Walt: What is it, Todd? Every time I talk to you, you act as
if...as if you wish I'd get lost.

Todd: Sorry.

Walt: Come on, don't be sorry.

Todd: I'm sor — I mean, OK.

Walt: All right.(*Looking into the classroom and laughing.*)
They should make the class periods five minutes longer,
just for Mrs. Johnson. She's always late coming out of
there. I had her last year, and it was the same thing.

Todd: Maybe, she... (*His voice trails off.*)

Walt: Maybe she what?

Todd: Nothing, it's nothing.

Walt: Look, Todd, we're not in peer counseling class yet. And even so, maybe I'm out of line. But I want to tell you something.

Todd: Yeah, what is it?

Walt: Why are you taking this class?

Todd: I don't understand.

Walt: The peer counseling class. There must be a reason. I mean, you sit there every day, and almost never open your mouth. And—

Todd: OK, OK! (*He stops abruptly and shakes his head.*)

Walt: What is it? What's wrong?

Todd: (*His voice breaking.*) I don't know what's wrong with me. I try, but...

Walt: Try what, Todd?

Todd: (*Sighing.*) It's so easy for you.

Walt: What is?

Todd: I must be some kind of freak. I don't know.

Walt: I can't help you if you don't let me know what's bothering you.

Todd: I don't have any friends. I can't make any friends. (*Shaking his head.*) The other school I went to, Lincoln, I mean, a had friends. Not many, but...

Walt: ...but you don't have friends here, is that it?

Todd: Yeah. It's hard for me.

Walt: Why? Why is it hard?

Todd: I don't know. Nobody wants to like me. I don't understand.

Walt: (*Sighs.*) Can I tell you something?

Todd: I guess.

Walt: Maybe you don't see it yourself. Maybe you aren't even aware of it. But it's like you're telling everyone to keep their distance.

Todd: I never —

Walt: I don't mean with words. But maybe that's part of the problem. Words, I mean. You hardly ever use them. And when you do... Look, what I'm trying to say is that your body language, the way you talk, everything is telling everyone else to keep back. I don't know why. Maybe, like you say, you don't know yourself. But half the battle is figuring it out.

Todd: I want friends. Everyone wants friends.

Walt: Most people, at any rate.

Todd: Are you implying I don't?

Walt: Part of you does, maybe. But part of you doesn't. Or there wouldn't be all the "hands off" signals you're giving. (*Pause.*) Maybe you're scared. Maybe you're afraid that, for some reason, the other kids will reject you. That I'll reject you. But I won't.

Todd *frowns in puzzlement.*

Walt: What I mean is, we're talking now. You took a chance, a really big risk in telling me. And I didn't reject you. I didn't tell you to buzz off. I can't say everyone else will respond the same way, but most people will. (*Pause.*) You're OK. You seem like...well, like a nice kind of guy. Most people, I think, will accept that. But nobody is liked by everyone.

Todd: You make it sound pretty simple. Being friendly, making friends.

Walt: It's not. Like I said, it takes risk. Maybe even commitment, you know.

Todd: But I can't just magically change the way I am.

Walt: No, you can't. But you can make a start.

Questions for Discussion

1. Do you think Todd really wants friends?

2. How do you feel about Walt's talking so frankly to him?

3. Why do you think Todd confides in Walt?

4. Walt asks, "Why? Why is it hard?" When practicing good communication, "Why?" questions are avoided. Discuss the reason for avoiding "Why?" questions, and see if it applies in this situation.

5. Walt says, "But you can make a start." Do you think Todd will?

Interfaith Dating

Scene i

The action occurs in the Goldstein's living room.

Myrna: It's not like we're planning to get married or anything. Loren asked me out on a date, that's all. What's wrong with that?

Mom: So far as I'm concerned, there's nothing wrong. But it's your father. You know how he feels. And even more so, your grandparents. They think it's wrong. To keep the peace, I wish you'd reconsider.

Myrna: I don't see why I should.

Mom: I've just told you.

Myrna: You've met Loren, remember? He was here the day we were planning the float decorations for Homecoming.

Mom: I remember.

Myrna: And I remember that you said you liked him. You said he seemed like "a nice boy."

Mom: No one said he wasn't.

Myrna: Then why can't I go out with him?

Mom: I didn't say you couldn't. I said that I hoped you wouldn't. Especially with your grandparents visiting. How do you think it will look to them?

Myrna: That I'm friends with — oh, horror of horrors — a gentile. A goy!

Mom: All right, Myrna. That's enough.

The lights fade.

Scene ii

The lights come up in the McNamara household.

Loren: You'd think I proposed marriage or something. What is this, anyhow?

Grandpa: In my day, we never even thought of such things.

Loren: Really, Grandpa? I know a lot of mixed marriages, as a matter of fact. People your age and older.

Grandma: Not very nice people, I must say. One shouldn't stray to other pastures, that's what I've always thought.

Loren: It's just a date. We're going to go to a movie and stop somewhere afterward.

Grandma: For something to eat?

Loren: Yes.

Grandma: This girl probably won't be able to do that. It won't be kosher.

Loren: Oh, for heaven's sake. Her family's not strict.

Grandpa: You mean they don't even believe enough in their own religion to practice it.

Loren: That isn't what I mean. For gosh sakes, Grandpa, you're not a fundamentalist either.

Grandma: Well, I don't think you should see this...what's her name?

The lights fade.

Scene iii

The lights come up on two separate areas. In one, **Myrna** *holds a phone to her ear. In the other,* **Loren** *also holds a phone. They are talking to each other.*

Myrna: I can't believe this.

Loren: I know what you mean. I think it's ridiculous. I tried to tell my grandma and grandpa that we're just going on a date. That we're just friends.

Myrna: I had the exact same conversation with my mother.

Loren: And even if it were more than that, so what?

Myrna: Maybe they have a point. I don't know. All those years of tradition. And my grandparents are pretty strict on all the rules and laws. Every time they come to see us, we have to do all sorts of things we wouldn't do otherwise.

Loren: Isn't that...a little dishonest?

Myrna: I suppose, but it keeps the peace. And even so, my dad agrees with a lot of their beliefs. He doesn't make an issue of it around Mom. Like observing the sabbath and that kind of thing.

Loren: Well, I don't have that choice, since I live with my grandparents. I think they're old-fashioned, too. But I still care a lot about them. I wouldn't want to make them feel bad. I wouldn't want to hurt them.

Myrna: I wouldn't want to hurt my family, either. It's a matter of scruples, isn't it?

Loren: We're still on, aren't we?

Myrna: Loren?

Loren: Yes?

Myrna: Never mind. (*Pause.*) You're picking me up about 7:45?

Loren: Right. I'll see you then.

Myrna: Sure. I'll see you then.

> **Myrna** *and* **Loren** *slowly and thoughtfully replace the receivers as the lights fade to black.*

Questions for Discussion

1. Discuss the reasons why Myrna's grandparents would not want her to have a date with Loren. Make a list of the reasons.

2. Make a list of the reasons why Loren's grandparents would not want him to date Myrna. Compare this list with the first one. What are the similarities? The differences?

3. What do you think Myrna wants to say to Loren before she hangs up?

4. What problems do people of different religious backgrounds encounter when they marry? How can they overcome these problems? Or can they?

5. Do you think Myrna and Loren keep their date? Why or why not?

SCHOOL

Having a Part-Time Job

The action takes place in a peer counseling class.

Alexandra: My parents say I have to quit my part-time job.

Eldon: Did they give a reason?

Alexandra: (*Sighs.*) Yes, they did.

Eldon: Well, what is it?

Alexandra: My dad said that if my grades aren't up this semester, I'll have to quit.

Todd: And the grades were pretty bad, huh?

Alexandra: That's an understatement.

Winston: Why were your grades so bad?

Alexandra: School's boring, you know? I hate it. I can't wait to get out.

Todd: I thought you were the *big brain*. Advanced English, math, and science.

Alexandra: Yeah, sure. I didn't ask to be put there.

Carla: I thought if you took advanced classes, you could skip some beginning college classes.

Alexandra: That's right.

Carla: So, what's the problem?

Alexandra: What's the problem? I told you, I hate school. I can't wait to get out.

Winston: To do what?

Alexandra: I don't know. Get a better job.

Todd: You don't want to go to college?

Alexandra: I haven't told many people this, but I want to be a comedienne, all right?

Winston: I think you already are.

Alexandra: Oh, yeah?

Winston: You're the fastest person with a comeback I've ever known.

Todd: Alex, you know what? You sound like you're really down today.

Alexandra: I suppose. Like I say, my parents told me I have to quit my job.

Winston: And the job's important to you.

Alexandra: You bet it is.

Todd: Why?

Alexandra: That's pretty apparent, isn't it?

Todd: I guess, but not to me.

Alexandra: The money, man. You dig?

Carla: What's behind all this?

Alexandra: Like I said, it's my job. I have to quit.

Carla: But you knew that if your schoolwork suffered you'd have to quit, right? And you still got bad grades. If you were put into three advanced classes, you must be pretty smart.

Alexandra shrugs.

Carla: So, what's the real problem?

Alexandra: I like my job. I can buy all kinds of things — stereo, tapes. My own TV. Clothes. I couldn't get them otherwise. Understand?

Several of the others nod.

Alexandra: There's no way I can go to college anyhow. So what's the point in trying to get good grades?

Winston: Why can't you go to college?

Alexandra: Five letters: M-O-N-E-Y. Money.

Todd: If you really want to go on to college, couldn't you save money from this job you have? What is it, anyhow?

Alexandra: I works in a concession stand, making *la-de-da* croissants. At *de mall.*

Todd: Why are you hiding, Alex?

Alexandra: What?

Todd: I mean, how you're reacting to all this.

Alexandra: (*Tears in her eyes.*) I really want to go to college. I really do.

Winston: I don't understand.

Alexandra: Mom and Dad don't have any money. I couldn't make it on my own.

Carla: What about loans and scholarships?

Alexandra: What about my grades? (*She shakes her head.*) I liked the money at my job. It was easy to work more and more hours. Then the grades started to slip. I told myself I'd bring them up, but it's too late. It's really too late.

Questions for Discussion

1. Why do you think Alexandra let her grades drop?

2. Do you think she really wants to go to college? Why or why not?

3. How important a part does her part-time job play in her situation?

4. As a peer counselor, how could you help her look at her options for going to college? List some of these options.

5. At first, Alexandra wears a mask to hide her true feelings. Why do you think she does this? In what other kinds of situations might people wear masks? Discuss different ways people protect themselves with masks.

The Question of College

The action takes place in the high school gym, just after cheerleading practice. **Annie** *and* **Colleen** *are sitting on the bleachers.*

Annie: I can't believe the last game's coming up this week.

Colleen: I know. I can't either. Pretty soon it'll be time for the prom, and then senior night and graduation.

Annie: Do you know what you're going to do?

Colleen: After graduation?

Annie: Yeah. You're going on to college, aren't you?

Colleen: That's a real sore point, Annie, between my mom and dad. Dad doesn't think I need college. He says I'll just get married and start having kids. So, there's no use throwing money away on an education I'll never use.

Annie: You're kidding.

Colleen: I wish I were. I can't believe an attitude like that. Mom says she'll help me out, but I don't know where she'd get the money. But they have this stupid agreement.

Annie: Your mom and dad?

Colleen: Yeah. Dad provides the money for the boys to go to college. Mom provides money for me, if I go. But, like I said, Dad's against it. How outdated can you get?

Annie: What do you think will happen?

Colleen: I really don't know. Maybe it's silly, but I want to be an architect. There aren't many women architects, but that's what I want to be. That's why I took all those drafting courses.

Annie: Where are you going to go?

Colleen: I don't think I am. At least, not right away. Mom has a little bit saved from jobs she's had, but not much. Not nearly enough, even for the first year. Yeah, I could get some loans, but I don't want to start out in debt when I finish. I just don't like that. Getting started will be hard enough as it is. So I'm going to try to get a job and live at home. Rent will be cheaper. And I'll save as much as I can. Maybe, in a couple of years, I can think about college. I'd like to go to Cincinnati. They have a good reputation.

Annie: Have you applied there?

Colleen: And six other places, too. I've been accepted at all of them. I had been hoping that it would work out somehow.

Annie: I wish we could change places.

Colleen: What do you mean?

Annie: My problem's just the opposite. I don't want to go to school anymore. I'm sick of school. I can get a good job right away at the *Tribune*, where my dad works. In the circulation department.

Colleen: So, what's the problem?

Annie: My parents. They've drummed it into my head all my life that I should go to college. They even started a savings account for tuition when I was in kindergarten. Can you imagine that?

Colleen: Have you told them how you feel?

Annie: I've tried. But they don't want to listen. They were never able to go to college themselves, and they both regretted it. Dad wanted to be an attorney. Mom wanted to be a teacher. They came from big families and started working right away.

Colleen: So, what's going to happen?

Annie: I don't know. I don't want to start and then drop out. I don't want to waste their money. But I don't want to go, either, at least not now. Later, maybe, I don't know. It might be fun to take some courses.

Colleen: What about your future?

Annie: Rod and I plan to get married in just another year. I'll keep working at the paper — if my parents will let me take the job — and Rod will go to city college.

Colleen: Will your parents accept that?

Annie: No, I really don't think they will. They've made me apply to lots of schools. And I've been accepted. But, darn it, just because I get good grades in high school shouldn't mean I have to go on.

Colleen: I'd give almost anything to be in your shoes.

Annie: I know what you mean.

Questions for Discussion

1. Compare Colleen's and Annie's situations. How do the attitudes of the parents differ?

2. What could Colleen do to make college a reality in the coming year?

3. Annie said she made good grades and was accepted at colleges. Why do you think she isn't interested in going? Do you think she is making a mistake? Why or why not?

4. If a counselee asks you to help him or her brainstorm the pros and cons of going to college, what would be some of the pros? Some of the cons?

5. Colleen and Annie mention they would like to change places. Use your imagination and allow them to do this. Pretend a year has gone by, and tell the class what each girl is doing.

Cheating in School

Scene i

The action occurs in a high school classroom where **Mr. Richardson** *is passing out copies of an exam.*

Mr. Richardson: I'm sure some of you will think it's unfair. And maybe it is, but I know for certain that two or three of you cheated when you took the exam last week.

Toni *raises her hand.*

Mr. Richardson: Yes, Toni?

Toni: Well, some of us didn't cheat, so why do all of us have to take it over?

There are murmurs of "That's right" from the rest of the class.

Mr. Richardson: Good point. The only thing I can say is that I'm trying to inject a little fairness into an unfair situation.

Kyle: What does that mean?

Mr. Richardson: (*Sighing.*) It means just what I said. This is a second chance for everyone. If you didn't cheat and you studied for last week's exam, your score should be essentially the same.

Alex: The facts were fresh in my mind then, Mr. Richardson. Now they're not.

Kyle: That's right. All of us— (*He looks around the classroom and grins.*) I take that back. *Most* of us studied the night before. I know I, for one, have probably forgotten some of the things I knew then.

Mr. Richardson: I'll take that into consideration.

Alex: How are you going to do that?

Mr. Richardson: You wouldn't have forgotten everything. So, if your score is close to the old one—within three or four points—I'll give you the same grade. And if it's higher, I'll give you the better grade.

Bob: I still don't think it's fair.

Mr. Richardson: In what way?

Bob: Why should we have to take the exam over?

Mr. Richardson: It's the only way I can have concrete proof of wrongdoing. If anyone's score is a lot lower this time, I'll know he or she cheated the first time.

Bob: I don't like to take exams. I'll bet no one in the class does. I don't like your forcing us into it. I want my old grade.

Toni: (*Under her breath.*) I'll bet you do.

Bob: (*Turning to her.*) Did you say something?

Toni *merely shrugs.*

Bob: What if I refuse to take the exam?

Mr. Richardson: The answer should be obvious.

Bob: You'll fail me, is that it?

Mr. Richardson: No. Rather, you'll be failing yourself.

Bob: Don't I have any rights?

Mr. Richardson: Come on, Bob, knock it off. You're just going to have to retake the exam.

The lights fade to black.

Scene ii

The lights come up again out in the hall after class.
Kyle *and* **Toni** *are talking*
as they walk to their next class.

Kyle: So, who do you think was cheating?

Toni: It's pretty apparent who *one* of them was.

Kyle: Who?

Toni: The one who complained the loudest.

Kyle: Bob?

Toni: Who else?

Kyle: How do you know that?

Toni: Have you ever known Bob Peoples to get a nearly perfect score before on anything? Anything at all?

Kyle: That's what he got?

Toni: I saw his paper.

Kyle: I wonder how he did it.

Toni: That's pretty obvious, too.

Kyle: What do you mean?

Toni: Richardson always gives the same exams to each of his sections. Bob got one of his friends to sneak an extra copy or something.

Kyle: And he copied the answers.

Toni: (*Shrugs.*) I'm sure we haven't heard the end of this, either. I can just see Bob and his friends reacting.

Kyle: It's like that time Lillian Harris and George Bishop had identical answers on their homework assignment, and Miss Dansinger accused them of cheating.

Toni: I remember. Lillian's mom wrote a note that even though she and George were going together, they would never cheat on their assignments.

Kyle: Which only proved that they did.

Toni: What I don't like is that, in effect, we were all being punished, like making the whole class stay after school because one person stole something.

Kyle: What else could Richardson do?

Questions for Discussion

1. Do you agree with Mr. Richardson that the entire class should take the examination again? Why or why not?

2. Why do you think Bob protested so loudly?

3. How do you feel about Toni and Kyle for suspecting Bob? Do you think they could have been wrong?

4. What else could Mr. Richardson have done?

5. Discuss famous people who have been caught cheating and the effect it has had on their careers.

Getting Along with Teachers

Scene i

The action takes place in a high school history class.
Jodie *opens the door and enters late.*

Ms. Robbins: Is there anyone who doesn't have a book yet for the next report?

Polly: I wanted to do something about Sherman's march, but I can't seem to find anything about it.

Ms. Robbins: Well, it just so happens I was in the bookstore over at State last Friday and saw this new book —

Jodie: (*Entering.*) Ms. Robbins, I need you to sign my admit slip.

Ms. Robbins: Just wait a minute, Jodie, will you please?

Jodie: You have to sign it, or I can't get in.

Ms. Robbins: (*Sighing.*) I'm aware of school policy, Jodie. I said I'd sign it, if you wait a minute.

Jodie: Miss Reynolds.

Ms. Robbins: What?

Jodie: I said, "Miss Reynolds." I want you to call me Miss Reynolds.

Ms. Robbins: Take your seat, Jodie.

Jodie acts as if she hasn't heard.

Ms. Robbins: I said, I want you to take your seat.

Jodie: (*Turning slowly toward her.*) Were you speaking to me?

Ms. Robbins: Take your seat right now.

Jodie: If I have to call you Ms. Robbins, then you have to call me Miss Reynolds. Well, *Ms. Robbins*, I want you to sign my admit slip.

Ms. Robbins: And I want you to shut your damn mouth.

Jodie: What? What did you say to me?

Ms. Robbins: You heard what I said.

The lights fade to black.

Scene ii

The lights come up on the kitchen of the Reynolds' house. **Jodie** *is drinking a glass of juice when her father enters.*

Jodie: Do you know what Ms. Robbins did today?

Dad: I'm afraid to ask.

Jodie: She refused to sign my admit slip.

Dad: (*Mildly.*) Why would she do that?

300

Jodie: Because she's a jerk, Dad.

Dad: There has to be more to it than that.

Jodie: She doesn't like me.

Dad: (*Sarcastically.*) But she's *your* favorite teacher, right?

Jodie: I can't stand her.

Dad: It's become the high point of my day, hearing stories about Ms. Robbins.

Jodie: Today she told me to shut my "damn mouth."

Dad: She did what?

Jodie: She told me to shut —

Dad: I heard you, Jodie. I was just surprised.

The phone rings.

Dad: (*Picking up the receiver.*) Hello?

The lights come up on a small area Stage Right, where **Ms. Robbins** *is seen talking on the phone.*

Ms. Robbins: Mr. Reynolds?

Dad: That's right.

Ms. Robbins: This is Adele Robbins, Jodie's history teacher.

Dad: Oh? Jodie and I were just discussing you.

Ms. Robbins: Quite frankly, Mr. Reynolds, I'm at my wit's end with Jodie.

Dad: I think you'd better explain.

Ms. Robbins: (*Sighs.*) All right. Last week, Jodie asked to close the window. She said she was cold.

Dad: And?

Ms. Robbins: I told her I thought it was really quite comfortable. She replied that she had a cold, and she didn't want to get chilled.

Dad: Sounds sensible.

Ms. Robbins: Maybe, but that isn't the point. I told her she could move to another desk. She said she didn't want to and asked again that I close the window. I told her I thought it would be too stuffy. Then she went into her little routine.

Dad: What do you mean by that?

Ms. Robbins: She said that she was sure I wanted her to get pneumonia. And so she'd sit by the window and get pneumonia. And then she'd die. And when she died, it would be all my fault.

Dad: Jodie told me all this.

Ms. Robbins: Then you can understand.

Dad: What I understand, Ms. Robbins, is that you and Jodie can't seem to get along. There's this big personality clash.

Ms. Robbins: I'm trying to do my best.

Dad: I'm sure that you are. But Jodie told me something today that I can't overlook.

Ms. Robbins: What can I say? I lost my temper.

Dad: Understandable, but —

Ms. Robbins: She insisted I call her Miss Reynolds.

Dad: What?

Ms. Robbins: She wouldn't acknowledge I was speaking to her unless I called her Miss Reynolds.

The lights fade.

Scene iii

The lights come up again in the Reynolds' kitchen. It's a few minutes later.

Dad: You really told her to call you Miss Reynolds?

Jodie: She's a jerk.

Dad: So you said. That still doesn't answer my question.

Jodie: She made me mad, OK?

Dad: And the bit about the window?

Jodie: Dad, it was cold. I was covered with goose bumps.

Dad: So, what are you going to do? The semester's barely started.

Questions for Discussion

1. Why do you think Jodie wants the teacher to call her Miss Reynolds?

2. What do you believe are Jodie's reasons for her confrontation with Ms. Robbins?

3. How do you feel about Ms. Robbins calling Jodie's father?

4. Do you think a teacher and student can work things out after they've clashed?

5. What are some of Jodie's options?

6. What are some of Ms. Robbins' options?

Being Too Laid Back

Scene i

The action takes place in the kitchen of the Carrothers house. **Jon** *is sitting at the table, across from his father.*

Mr. Carrothers: I don't understand you.

Jon *shrugs.*

Mr. Carrothers: Aren't you even going to answer me?

Jon: What do you want me to say?

Mr. Carrothers: I want a reaction. Lord, boy, any kind of reaction will do.

Jon: I'm sorry.

Mr. Carrothers: You're sorry.

Jon: That's what I said.

Mr. Carrothers: Your IQ is way up in the —. It's so doggone high, it almost goes off the scale. And you're flunking out of school. Can you tell me about that?

Jon *simply stares at his father.*

Mr. Carrothers: Don't you care about anything?

Jon: Yeah, I care.

Mr. Carrothers: What about, for heavens sake?

Jon: I don't know.

Mr. Carrothers: Not about school, that's for sure. I've tried everything I can think of. Putting you on restriction, rewarding good grades. Nothing helps. And it's not just school, it's everything. It's like you think if you ignore something — everything — then it will go away.

Jon: Maybe those things aren't important to me.

Mr. Carrothers: It's not important to stay in school? Maybe even go on to college?

Jon: If you say so.

Mr. Carrothers: If I say so, huh?

Jon: Can I go to my room now?

The lights dim.

Scene ii

It's after school. **Jon** *and his best friend,* **Quinn,** *are walking home together.*

Quinn: So, your dad really let you have it?

Jon: I suppose.

Quinn: So, what's the problem? I mean, why is he on your case?

Jon: He's says I'm too...laid back.

Quinn *laughs.*

Jon: Hey, Quinn, I don't need that. Not from you.

Quinn: A spark of anger? A real spark of anger?

Jon: (*Laughing.*) Destroys the image, huh?

Quinn: Look, Jon, did you ever think that maybe your dad is right?

Jon: (*Surprised.*) What are you talking about?

Quinn: I'm your best friend, right?

Jon: Sure.

Quinn: Then it's OK for me to tell you...

Jon: Tell me what?

Quinn: That you're messing up, man. Look, I know how much you like art class, for instance. And you're good.

Jon: So?

Quinn: So why'd you get an F this semester?

Jon: I... I didn't turn a lot of stuff in.

Quinn: And what you turned in you aced, right?

Jon: Yeah.

Quinn: Well?

Jon: I don't know. I can't answer you. Maybe it sounds dumb, but I really can't.

Quinn: I believe you. I've known you, what, since fifth grade?

Jon: Yeah.

Quinn: I think I know you pretty well. (*Shrugs.*) I guess it really isn't my business. But I remember that one time you were on restriction for a whole semester.

Jon: Yeah. Maybe I was trying to prove something. I don't know.

Quinn: What have you got to prove, man?

Jon: Nothing, I guess. OK?

Quinn: (*Punching him on the upper arm.*) OK.

Questions for Discussion

1. Does Mr. Carrothers listen to his son? Is he trying to help?

2. What are the reasons why people are laid back?

3. Do you think Jon wants to fail?

4. How could Mr. Carrothers handle the situation differently?

5. What do you think Jon is trying to prove?

6. Is Quinn a good friend? Could he do more?

Being an Exchange Student

The action takes place in a peer counseling class.

Olga: I never realized how important family traditions were. Not until this year. Being away from home at Christmastime makes me very sad.

Steve: I've never been away from home except for a few weeks in the summer. I guess I've always taken family and traditions for granted.

Amy: I'd be sad too, Olga, thousands of miles from home. (*Pause.*) Would it help to talk about your feelings?

Olga: When I first came to the United States, I was excited. It was wonderful to be in a different country, to go to a new school. But within a few weeks I began to feel homesick. The one thing that has helped is this class. I don't know what I'd have done without you. I'm fortunate to have you.

Amy: We're the lucky ones. You always seem to add a sparkle to the class.

Olga: I'm afraid I don't have any sparkle today. I thought after the initial homesickness, I'd be OK the rest of the year. I didn't count on December being like this.

Steve: Why don't you tell us about your traditions? It would be interesting. And talking about them might bring back nice memories for you.

Olga: My mother always cooks for weeks before Christmas. (*Smiling.*) The smells are wonderful. Each day, when I come home from school, I sit at the kitchen table and sample what Mother has baked that day. And I talk to her about school. She's a great listener. I don't think I realized that until we started learning about active listening. That's something Mom does instinctively.

Steve: She sounds very nice.

Olga: She is, and so is Dad. In a different way. He doesn't have much time to sit and listen because of his job. But he always takes his vacation during December, so he can help us buy the tree and decorate it. And we spend a whole day shopping.

Wanda: I can't imagine my dad shopping all day.

Olga: Oh, it isn't just shopping. It's a family outing. My parents, my sister, and I shop, have lunch and dinner at a restaurant, and then go to the theatre. We see *A Christmas Carol* or *The Nutcracker Ballet*. We don't get home till midnight—so tired we can hardly make it, but wonderfully happy.

Steve: I can see why you'd miss that. Will your family go this year without you?

Olga: Next week. I wish I could be home for that one day and for Christmas. Then I'd be ready to come back for the rest of the year.

Wanda: I can really relate to that feeling. I wish I could have just one more Christmas like I used to have with my family.

Olga: Your family won't be together this year?

Wanda: No, and really never again.

Steve: Would you like to tell us about it?

Wanda: Mom and Dad were divorced. Last summer. Now I have to choose who to spend Christmas with. I want to spend it with both of them. As a family, like every year I can remember.

Amy: That must be difficult. I wouldn't know which parent to choose.

Olga: I'm sorry, Wanda. Here I am complaining about being away for just one year. Your situation must be much more painful.

Wanda: It *is* painful. But we'll talk about it later. I didn't mean to interrupt. Please go ahead.

Olga: Your comments have given me a lot to think about. Somehow, I'm not feeling so sorry for myself anymore. Besides, my host family places a lot of emphasis on the holidays. So I'll be able to know American traditions, as well as those of my own country. Then next year, when I'm home with my family, I'll have new things to share. Maybe we'll even start a new tradition or two from something I've carried back from my trip.

Questions for Discussion

1. Discuss family traditions. Make a list of the ones you have in your home. Compare those with other class members' lists.

2. What things does Olga miss the most being away from home?

3. Discuss the feelings that Olga must have had when she arrived in a new country.

4. Compare Olga's and Wanda's situations. Which situation would be harder to live with?

5. List personal characteristics an exchange student must have in order to adjust to a new country, a new school, and new friends.

Leaving for College

The action takes place in a peer counseling class.

Mindy: I always thought I'd have my life all organized by the time senior year rolled around. I thought I'd know exactly what I wanted to do, and everything would fall into place.

Jeff: It sounds like things haven't gone that smoothly.

Mindy: You're right. And I don't know when they ever will.

Jean: Want to tell us about it?

Mindy: There's not much to tell. I wanted to go to college in Boston ever since I can remember. I worked hard to get the grades to be accepted.

Marshall: You probably study more than anyone else in this class. Like that time when the basketball team got to the finals. and you missed the championship game to study for a physics test. I don't have that kind of discipline. I don't think many people here do.

Mindy: I've given up a lot to keep my grade point average high enough.

Jean: What's the problem then? You won't have trouble being accepted, will you?

Mindy: No, I've already been accepted by two schools in Boston and one in California.

Jeff: That's great, Mindy. Congratulations.

Mindy: It isn't so great.

Jeff: I don't understand.

Mindy: When I was trying hard to get accepted, everything was fine with my mom. But when the acceptance letters came, her whole attitude changed.

Jean: Let me guess. She decided Boston was too far from home.

Mindy: How did you know?

Jean: I wanted to go to Florida. Suddenly, Mom began to think it was as far away as Japan.

Mindy: My brother and sister went to school close to home. So, I suppose I'll have to do the same thing.

Jean: Me, too. Three hundred miles instead of the other side of the country.

Mindy: You're lucky if you can get three hundred miles away.

Marshall: Can't you do that, too?

Mindy: Mother has decided that "it would be best" for me to go to a community college and live at home another year. She said that if I stay home for two more years, she'll give me the money I'll save not paying room and board. Then

I could buy a car to take with me for the last two years of college.

Marshall: How do you feel about that?

Mindy: The thought is tempting. But I still want to go to Boston. I've wanted to for years, ever since we went there on vacation.

Jean: Why does your mother want you at home?

Mindy: She gives me all kinds of reasons. She thinks I'll get homesick. I could only come home at Christmastime. She says I won't like the colder climate. Her reasons go on and on.

Marshall: It sounds like you think she's not telling you her real reasons.

Mindy: I know. (*Sighs.*) She doesn't want to be all by herself in a big, empty house.

Jean: I remember, your parents were divorced.

Mindy: (*Nods.*) Two years ago. And I want Mom to sell the house when I leave. She doesn't need all that space, and if she got a condo, she wouldn't have all that yardwork.

Marshall: Maybe she enjoys it.

Mindy: I think it's more the finality of selling the house.

Jean: Can you explain that?

Mindy: Mom seems to be holding on to the idea that someday Dad will come back and things will be the same as before. But he's not coming back. I wish she'd accept that.

Marshall: If she wants to keep the house the same, could she also want to keep the same people living in it?

Mindy: I'm not sure I know what you mean.

Marshall: Even if your dad came back, you wouldn't be there. Things could never be the same.

Mindy: Could be. But I'm sure she hates the thought of being alone. And I can't blame her.

Jean: It sounds like you really care about her.

Mindy: I do. She's great. She's always been so supportive — except when it comes to my going to Boston.

Jean: That makes your decision even harder, right?

Mindy: It sure does. I feel guilty, sometimes, about wanting to leave. But then I feel I should get to do what I want.

Marshall: It's a conflict between your mother's wants and your own.

Mindy: Yeah. And you know something? I've never been angry at my dad before for leaving, but now I am. And I don't like it. But I'm thinking if he were home, Mom wouldn't be on my case. And then I wouldn't feel guilty.

Questions for Discussion

1. Discuss the pros and cons of going to college a long distance from home.

2. Why do you think Mindy's mother does not want her to go to college in Boston? Should she have told Mindy earlier? Why or why not?

3. Should the parents, the student, or both decide where the student goes to college? Why?

4. Discuss some feelings Mindy's mother is probably having.

5. Mindy says she is angry with her father. Is this anger justified? Why or why not?

Senioritis

The action takes place in a peer counseling class.

Nora: I'm seeing three counselees right now. And you know, they all have the same problem.

Nike: Let me guess. I'm seeing two seniors, and neither wants to come to school. They'd rather spend time at the beach and not do homework. Is that it?

Nora: It sure is. "Senioritis." Everyone goes through it, I guess, at least a little. But these guys may not graduate.

Nike: Cutting too many classes?

Nora: Not only that, but not getting assignments in on time.

Wally: I can't believe anyone would get this far and then blow it.

Nora: You don't have any problems with studying; some people do.

Wally: I guess I wouldn't be a good peer counselor to the people you're seeing. I'd be impatient.

Nora: Well, I've been known to cut a few classes myself. But I'd never jeopardize my graduation.

Nike: I don't think most of us would. But there are a few who do.

Nora: And they usually wake up around the middle of May and realize the mess they're in.

Nike: And they start looking for a peer counselor.

Wally: Should you waste your time on these characters when other people out there have real problems?

Nike: They have real problems. Not graduating is pretty serious.

Nora: I feel the same. If we can help kids get their priorities straight, we're not wasting our time.

Wally: I guess so. I never looked at it that way before.

Nora: I think maybe senioritis is a big enough problem to start group sessions. What do you think?

Nike: Like we did for kids with drug and alcohol problems?

Nora: Something like that. Maybe two or three counselors to every ten counselees.

Nike: Sounds good. Particularly if we group them according to the kind of help they need.

Nora: Yeah, the ones having trouble with English term papers could meet with whomever's strong in English.

Wally: I like the idea. I think it'll work. The counselees could motivate each other. A kind of positive peer pressure.

Nora: Trying to make sure that the others in the group do their work to graduate.

Wally: They'd also be working at the same time, and wouldn't be tempted to skip sessions to meet with their friends.

Nora: Hey, Wally, you're coming up with so many interesting ideas, maybe you'd like to become involved.

Wally: I don't have anyone with that kind of problem.

Nora: It doesn't matter. Come in and help when we get stuck.

Wally: Maybe I need to learn to respect these characters.

Nike: You do a lot of peer tutoring already. I don't see that you have any problems with respecting people who need help.

Wally: The kids I've tutored need help because they have trouble understanding things. The ones we're talking about would probably understand the material. They just aren't in class to hear it.

Nike: Yeah, but we're not supposed to judge.

Questions for Discussion

1. What is senioritis?

2. Describe how Wally becomes motivated to work with students having senioritis.

3. What are the benefits of having several peer counselors work together instead of separately?

4. Discuss what it means to be nonjudgmental. Why do you think Wally has a difficult time learning this lesson?

5. List other ways to help the student suffering from senioritis.

Playing Favorites

The action takes place as two high school baseball players are walking home after a game.

Ben: Did you ever see anything like it?

Scott: You mean the way Coach Haymes played his son for the entire game?

Ben: I mean, did you ever see a player make so many errors in one game and not get benched? If it'd been anyone except Tony Haymes missing those fly balls, he'd have been replaced at the end of the second inning.

Scott: You're so right. Remember the coach pulled me two games ago when I struck out with a man on third?

Ben: (*Laughing.*) You have to admit that last ball you swung at was pretty high — and wide.

Scott: OK. So I deserved to sit out the rest of the game. I wouldn't mind that, if we were all treated the same. If Tony had been pulled today. But that's not what happens.

Ben: I know, and it wouldn't be so bad if we hadn't lost. But the whole time I kept thinking that Al could have helped us with a win. If the coach had sent him in.

Scott: Yeah, and just think how Al felt sitting on the bench watching Tony miss all those easy catches.

Ben: I don't know what we can do. We can't talk to Coach Haymes. No one can. Not where his son is concerned.

Scott: If only he could see how unfair it is. Not just to the rest of us, but Tony, too.

Ben: What do you mean? How's it unfair to Tony?

Scott: Didn't you see how everyone treated him afterwards? No one even talked to him.

Ben: I, for one, was too angry to try to say anything.

Scott: I felt the same way. But think how he must feel. He knows he played a lousy game. I'm sure he thinks the errors cost us a win. On top of that, he was totally ignored in the locker room.

Ben: Man, if that were me, I'd feel like just not showing up on the field anymore.

Scott: Me, too. But you know, it wasn't his fault. He's a darn good player. Everyone has off days.

Ben: If we were having an off day, Coach would take us right out. Particularly if we were losing.

Scott: True. But I'm willing to bet Coach Haymes will never replace his son.

Ben: Whew. And just think, we have the rest of the season in front of us.

Scott: If we can't talk to Coach Haymes, what about talking to Tony?

Ben: What good will that do?

Scott: For starters, we could let him know we're still his friends. If I were in his place, I'd feel like I didn't have a friend in the world.

Ben: Sure, that's fine. But it still doesn't solve the problem.

Questions for Discussion

1. How do you think Tony feels being favored by his father, the coach? How do you think he feels after the game, when the other players don't speak to him?

2. If you were on the team, how would you treat Tony?

3. Do Ben and Scott have a right to be upset? If they had won the game, do you think they would have felt differently?

4. What would Ben and Scott gain by talking to Tony?

SELF-ESTEEM

Low Self-Esteem

The action occurs in a peer counseling setting. A group of young people are present.
Matthew *is the focus of attention.*

Matthew: It's hard to talk about this. It's like I'm really ashamed of it. But I just feel I'm not worth anything.

Rhonda: Do you really feel that way? That you're not worth anything?

Matthew: Yeah, that I'm totally useless. Why would anyone like me or care about me? You know, sometimes when I'm really down, I start talking to myself. Out loud. When no one's around. Telling myself that I'm garbage, that I'm not worth...you know.

Rhonda: Obviously, that isn't true. I've known you for a couple of months now, right?

Matthew *nods.*

Rhonda: And I like you. You have a lot of good qualities.

Matthew: (*Dejectedly.*) Yeah, right.

Sam: You sound like you don't believe that, Matt.

Matthew: With my brain, maybe, I do. But it's like I'm two people. The other one, the one who makes me feel, he knows I'm not worth anything.

Rhonda: What about your accomplishments? You're in the school band, the honor society, and a lot of other things.

Matthew: (*Looking down, almost mumbling.*) A fluke.

Sam: (*Incredulous.*) Did you say what I think you did?

Matthew: I read this book a few years back. About "the impostor syndrome." Well, that's me.

Rhonda: What do you mean?

Matthew: (*Shrugs.*) I don't really play the trumpet that well. I'm not really smart. I'm not really good at anything. Sometimes people think I am, but I'm not.

Sam: I don't understand.

Matthew: Look, I'm smart enough to figure out what I'm doing, to analyze it. But I have no control over it. I rationalize my way out of everything. I play first chair in band just because my last name comes before anyone else's. I mean before any of the other trumpet players' names. So I'm thought of as first.

Rhonda: I used to be in band. You have auditions, right? Every once in a while.

Matthew: We used to.

Rhonda: Not anymore?

Matthew: Uh-uh. We're placed according to how Mr. Adams thinks of us.

Sam: So, then, he must think you're pretty good.

Matthew: But I'm not. Lot's of kids are better than me.

Sam: What kids?

Matthew: Where I take lessons. I've heard them. And besides...

Rhonda: What is it, Matthew? It sounds like something's really bothering you.

Matthew: This is really hard for me to say.

Sam: We're here to listen. It's a safe atmosphere, you know. Like in spy movies where they have a safe house. Well, this is your safe house.

Matthew: OK. My mom, she says no matter how hard I try, I can't ever be as good as my dad.

Rhonda: She actually said that?

Matthew: A lot of times. And not just about music. My dad came from a big family and had to work a lot on the farm, and he still got good grades. He took music lessons and was better than anyone else. He's the best at everything. And I can never come up to him. Never be as good as he is, no matter what I do.

Sam: Do you accept that as the truth, Matt?

Matthew: I guess I have to. It's what I've been told all my life. "You're not good enough. No matter what you do, you don't match up to your father."

Rhonda: Look, Matt, your parents are only human. Your father isn't some sort of superman.

Matthew: I realize that, but still...

Sam: How do you view yourself, Matt?

Matthew: What do you mean?

Sam: Everyone has good points and bad points.

Matthew: But you don't understand. I feel I have to be the best at everything.

Rhonda: In competition with your father.

Matthew: I guess so. And I have to do it on his terms, even though I know I can't match up.

Sam: On his terms? What does that mean?

Matthew: Like I said, my dad had to work hard as a teenager. He didn't have much time for schoolwork. So, you see, I tell myself I have to get high grades with very little work.

Rhonda: Could your father be exaggerating?

Matthew: What do you mean?

Rhonda: Maybe not even consciously. But looking back, we add our own feelings and, well, judgments I guess, to the memories. Maybe his grades weren't so high. Maybe he did have more time for study than he remembers.

Matthew: (*Shrugging.*) Maybe.

Rhonda: You don't sound convinced.

Matthew: But no matter what, I can't be as good as he is. Especially in music.

Sam: If you really think that's the case, why do you try?

Matthew: That's a good question.

Sam: You mean, you don't know.

Matthew: (*Managing to laugh.*) I don't know.

Questions for Discussion

1. What would you do if someone like Matthew came to you for help?

2. List characteristics of persons having low self-esteem. Make another list of persons with high self-esteem. Compare the two lists.

3. If you decided to refer Matthew to someone else, what kind of professional help would you recommend?

4. Why do you think Matthew's mother compares him to his father?

Physical Appearance

The action occurs in a peer counseling setting.

Sharon: I've been putting this off for a long time. But there's something I really need to talk about. (*Pause.*) It's about the way I look.

Corey: What about it?

Sharon: (*Snapping at him.*) That should be pretty obvious. (*Sighs.*) I'm sorry. It's my problem, not yours.

Corey: That doesn't mean you have to try to handle it alone.

Amy: What did you want to say, Sharon?

Sharon: I'm over — . No, I'm fat, just plain fat.

Amy: And it bothers you.

Sharon: Wouldn't it bother you? (*Sighs.*) Do you think I like wearing...tents? Nothing I wear ever looks right. I can't...

Corey: What, Sharon? What can't you do?

Sharon: No matter what I do, I can't lose any weight. I've tried. Everything you can think of.

Corey: And nothing works?

Sharon: Maybe it would, except that every time any little thing goes wrong, there I am, at the refrigerator, stuffing in food.

Amy: Any idea why that happens?

Sharon: No. Yes. I've read the articles. I know it's to feel security, comfort. Except that it isn't secure or comfortable. Not for long. In a little while, I start to feel guilty and depressed. I hate myself. And then I start to feel this terrible hunger again.

Amy: Have you tried things like Weight Watchers?

Sharon: Overeaters Anonymous. I tried that. But everyone was two or three times older than I am. And I started to think, "Is that what's in store for me?"

Corey: So you dropped out.

Sharon: You know the worst thing? It's how other people treat you. The things they say that are supposed to be funny.

Sterling: I can really identify with that, you know.

Sharon: Oh?

Sterling: Look at me. No matter what, I can't gain. I hate people calling me a bean pole and all kinds of other things. I can't gain. I'm always eating and...and nothing happens.

Corey: I never realized you felt that way.

Amy: What can you do about it? What can either of you do about it?

Sterling: It seems to me, Sharon, that yours is at least partly an emotional problem.

Sharon: I know.

Sterling: So, if you start accepting yourself, if you can somehow stop letting problems throw you so much, maybe there's a chance, then, that you'll start to lose.

Sharon: Maybe. But you know what?

Sterling: What?

Sharon: It's the same kind of thing with you.

Sterling: Oh?

Sharon: I don't mean you can gain weight or anything. But you said part of my problem is emotional, that I need to accept myself. The same could be true of you. If you can tell yourself, "OK. I'm thin, and that's the way it is. I can't do anything about it, but it's not so bad, and otherwise I'm a pretty good guy..." See what I mean, Sterling?

Sterling: Easier said than done.

Sharon: I know that. From lots of experience, I know.

Amy: You two have a lot going for you. The weight is just one part of the total person. Not even that important a part.

Corey: Self-acceptance is sometimes a pretty hard thing to accomplish.

Sharon: It sure is.

Questions for Discussion

1. Do the peer counselors make a mistake in not referring Sharon to a professional?

2. Do you think Sharon will stay on a diet without dealing with her guilt and depression?

3. Does Sterling really understand Sharon's problem?

4. Do you think the peer counselors should have helped Sterling discover alternatives?

5. How do you feel when Amy says, "The weight is just one part of the total person. Not even that important a part." Do you agree or disagree?

SEXUALLY TRANSMITTED DISEASES

Finding Out Too Late

The action occurs in the Thompson's living room.

Tammy: I'm sorry. I'm really sorry.

Dad: I'm glad you told me about it, but I don't know what to say. You can understand that, can't you?

Tammy: I never thought...

Dad: I know. But what's done is done.

Tammy: The doctor said she wants to see me again in a month. She prescribed all these pills. Grandpa loaned me the money. Sixty dollars. How am I going to pay him back?

Dad: We'll work it out, OK?

Tammy: Can you die from it, Dad?

Dad: From gonorrhea? No, I don't think so.

Tammy: She said I might've had it for a long time. With girls, you can't tell. It doesn't always show up right away.

Dad: You know, Tammy, I really don't want to talk about this.

Tammy: You're ashamed of me, aren't you?

Dad: No, I'm not... Maybe I am, Tammy. I don't know. I can't help my feelings.

Tammy: If Mom were still alive, I wonder what she'd say. She'd be so disappointed.

Dad: I don't know.

Tammy: But she would, wouldn't she?

Dad: Tammy, I can't answer that. All I can say is, I love you. No matter what, I still love you. I just wish...

Tammy: It was only one time, Dad. Just one time, you know?

Dad: I don't know what you ever saw in that character.

Tammy: You're jumping to conclusions. How do you know it was Andrew?

Dad: Wasn't it? Who else do you know...?

Tammy: Who would give me gonorrhea? Is that what you mean?

Dad: I guess so.

Tammy: What if I told you it was someone else? What if I said it was Scott? You're so sure, though. You think you know so much about it.

Dad: Was it Scott?

Tammy *doesn't answer.*

Dad: Well, was it?

Tammy: It was Andrew.

Dad: You told them who it was, didn't you? At the doctor's office. I mean, you said it was Andrew.

Tammy: I couldn't do that.

Dad: But you have to. That's the law. Or, at least, it used to be.

Tammy: They asked me. (*Starting to cry.*) Oh, Daddy, I didn't even tell you the worst part.

Dad: What do you mean?

Tammy: Afterwards, when Dr. Simmons was talking to me. She said... She said I'll never be able to have any kids.

Dad: Oh, honey, I'm sorry.

Tammy: It went on too long, or something. That makes me really sad, you know? It was just one mistake, Daddy. And I'll have to pay for it all my life.

Questions for Discussion

1. True or False: Tammy and her dad seem to communicate well. Discuss your reasons for the choice.

2. Tammy's dad tells her he loves her. How important is that for her to hear? Why?

3. List some social diseases and their symptoms.

4. Discuss some of the long-term effects of having a social disease.

5. How can high school students be better informed about these diseases before it is too late?

Having Herpes

The action takes place at the front door of Bonnie's house. **Tiffany** *rings the doorbell and* **Bonnie** *answers.*

Tiffany: I could kill him!

Bonnie: What's wrong, Tiffany? I've never seen you so upset.

Tiffany: Upset doesn't begin to describe how I feel.

Bonnie: Come on in and tell me what happened.

*The girls enter the hallway
and cross to Bonnie's bedroom.*

Tiffany: I hope your parents didn't hear me talking when you opened the door. I wouldn't want them to know about this.

Bonnie: They aren't home. Now, tell me what's wrong.

Tiffany: I just came from my doctor's office. I have an STD.

Bonnie: A what?

Tiffany: STD stands for Sexually Transmitted Disease. STD, for short.

Bonnie: Oh, no. Do you have syphilis?

Tiffany: Herpes. Now do you see why I feel like killing Dennis?

Bonnie: I'm glad you came here before you talked to him.

Tiffany: Who said I was going to talk to him?

Bonnie: I understand why you're upset, but try to think through this rationally.

Tiffany: There's nothing to think about. It's done.

Bonnie: How do you know Dennis gave it to you?

Tiffany: What?! You don't think I've been with...

Bonnie: I just asked a question.

Tiffany: You know I haven't had sex with anyone else. I never slept with him till just a few months ago. I told you about the first time. Remember? It was after the senior prom.

Bonnie: I remember how scared you were that you might get pregnant.

Tiffany: I should have learned my lesson and stopped having sex. But, oh, no, I just kept on.

Bonnie: Are you sure you didn't get it some other way?

Tiffany: Besides having sex, you mean?

Bonnie: Yes.

Tiffany: My doctor told me that I have Herpes Simplex Type II. You get it by having sex.

Bonnie: That means that Dennis has it, too. He'll be upset when he finds out.

Tiffany: I hadn't thought of that. I guess I'm still too angry to care about his feelings.

Bonnie: You'll have to tell him, so he can be treated.

Tiffany: I'll tell him. I'll tell him we're finished, too.

Bonnie: I know how much you like Dennis. Maybe you'd better think it over, at least till tomorrow.

Tiffany: Do you think I'd go with a boy again who's been with some other girl? A girl who gave him herpes? Maybe he's even been seeing her when...when we've been seeing each other.

Bonnie: It would be all over school if he were. You know he's not.

Tiffany: The only thing I know is that I trusted Dennis, and look where it got me.

Bonnie: I guess I'm naive. But what exactly does herpes do? What are the symptoms?

Tiffany: There are sores, but the doctor says they'll go away. The trouble is, they could flare up at any time. I'm also more likely now to get cervical cancer, and I could have problems with a pregnancy. How's that for making a person feel great?

Bonnie: I didn't know it was so serious. I'm sorry, Tiffany. I'm really sorry.

Tiffany: I'm too angry now to feel sorry, but I'm sure I will later.

Bonnie: I'm sure you'll start thinking, why did it have to be you?

Tiffany: Maybe. But the hardest to answer will be: Why didn't I wait to have sex? (*Starting to cry.*) I didn't need to take chances, did I?

Questions for Discussion

1. What does STD stand for? Give some examples of an STD.

2. Make a list of feeling words that would describe Tiffany when she found she had herpes.

3. What may be some long-range effects of having herpes?

4. Tiffany questions why she took chances. What are some ways to say "no" to having sex while in high school?

5. Do you think Dennis will be as upset as Tiffany was? Describe what he might feel.

SUICIDE

Planning Suicide

Scene i

The action occurs in the high school locker room. The home team has just lost a hard-fought game. All the players have left except Howard and Jim. Jim is tying his shoelace as Howard slams his basketball shoes hard into the door of a metal locker.

Jim: (*Turning to* **Howard.**) Hey, man, cut that out. Throwing things isn't going to help.

Howard: The problem is, nothing's going to help.

Jim: OK, it was an important game, and we lost. It's not the end of the world.

Howard: (*Softly, as if to himself.*) I wish it were.

Jim closes his locker and crosses to Howard. He sits beside Howard and places a hand on his shoulder.

Jim: So you missed some shots. Everyone has off-nights.

Howard: It's not the game I'd like to forget. It's my life.

Jim: Things are bad, huh?

Howard: They sure are.

Jim: Hey, look, they'll be closing things up here. Why don't we go grab a burger and fries? (*He pauses.*) We can talk.

Howard *shrugs.*

Jim: (*Ignoring the body language.*) Good, let's go.

The lights fade to black.

Scene ii

The lights quickly come up again. **Jim** *and* **Howard** *sit at a small table. A waitress serves them hamburgers and soft drinks.*

Howard: (*Looking away from* **Jim**.) You can't understand. You haven't been there.

Jim: Maybe not. But why don't you try me?

Howard: (*With a resigned tone.*) Too bad we never really got to know each other off the basketball court. But I know you're one of those counselors or whatever.

Jim: A peer counselor. Yeah.

Howard: I don't know if talking's going to help or not. But maybe I just need someone to listen, at least tonight.

Jim: OK.

Howard: People keep saying I have it all — grades, popularity, maybe a basketball scholarship...

Jim: Yes?

Howard: But they don't understand. No one understands. I don't have it all. I... I don't have things that matter.

Jim: Like what?

Howard: Like a family that cares. Like a father who would miss one — just one — so-called "important business meeting" to see me play. Like a mother who would stay sober until I got home from school.

Jim: I never knew, Howie.

Howard: No one does.

Jim: But your family always seemed...like the ideal family. What every family should be. A beautiful house, the whole bit.

Howard: Maybe it looks that way.

Jim: You'll be going away in a couple of months. To college. You can leave all this behind.

Howard: But that's just it. I can't leave. I realized that earlier this week. I can't go to college. I can't leave Mom. Man, I came home from basketball practice on Monday and found her passed out on the sofa. A cigarette had dropped out of her hand and was burning a hole in the rug. She could have burned up everything, herself included.

Jim: Did you tell your father?

Howard: Sure. But it didn't do any good. He just told me to keep an eye on her. He's disgusted with her drinking.

Jim: And?

Howard: It's more than I can handle. If I'm not around, then he'll have to take the responsibility.

Jim: Sorry, Howard, I'm afraid you lost me. I thought you said you couldn't go away. That college was out.

Howard: I did say that. If I left, I'd still be involved.

Jim: What did you mean, then, about not being around?

Howard: (*Becoming agitated.*) Do I have to draw you a picture?

Jim: You mean you're thinking of suicide.

Howard: Smart. You're the one who should go to college.

Jim: Have you made plans...about how you're going to do this?

Howard: Yeah, you know me. I always plan ahead.

Jim: Tell me about it.

Howard: (*Shrugs.*) I planned to do it this weekend. But after tonight, I want to play one more game. I don't want people to remember me as playing a lousy last game. I couldn't do anything right tonight.

Jim: Have you thought of how you're going to do it?

Howard: I sure have. I thought of pills. Some of Mom's. But that doesn't always work. A gun's more final.

Jim: Do you have access to a gun?

Howard: Dad keeps one in his nightstand. Ever since we were robbed a couple of years ago. (*Laughs.*) He doesn't bother to lock it up.

Jim: Where would you do it?

Howard: I'd drive away from home. A couple of blocks. Pull over to the curb, and that's it.

Jim: You wouldn't do it at home?

Howard: Naw. It would freak out my sister if she found me.

Jim: You want someone other than family to find your body?

Howard: (*Sighs.*) It will be easier that way. The police will cruise by, see me slumped over the wheel, and stop. They'll take me to the morgue before my family even knows. Everything will be neat and tidy.

Jim: It seems like you have it all planned out. Down to the last detail.

Howard: I sure have. I lie awake at night and visualize the whole thing. I was going to give my things away this weekend. But I want to play another game, now. So I won't be in a rush to get rid of my stuff.

Jim: What are you giving away?

Howard: Things that matter to me. My stereo goes to Bill, camera to Helen, fishing rod to Randy.

Jim: Look, Howard. I'd really like to talk some more, but it's getting kind of late. Can we talk again tomorrow night?

Howard: If you want to.

Jim: Yes, I do. Will you promise me that you'll wait until after the game this next week before you do anything?

Howard: Sure. I told you I want to play again — my kind of game this time.

Jim: That's good, Howie. I do care about you, and I want us to talk tomorrow night.

Howard: Fine.

Jim: How about meeting here again? About eight o'clock?

Howard: OK.

Questions for Discussion

1. Is Howard serious about killing himself? What makes you think he is or isn't?

2. Does Jim identify with Howard at any time? Why?

3. Is Jim correct in asking Howard if he intends to kill himself?

4. Should Jim stay with Howard that night? Why or why not?

5. What are Howard's feeling toward his family? Explain.

6. If you were Jim, how would you handle the situation?

7. Why is Howard giving away his favorite possessions?

Expectations Too High

The action takes place on the front steps of the school, shortly after the dismissal bell. **Spence** *and* **Peggy** *are waiting for her mother to pick them up.* **Hal** *has stopped just to talk.*

Hal: You heard about Burke, didn't you? Isn't it awful?

Peggy: To kill yourself like that. He must have been... I don't know. He just went off the deep end.

Hal: I don't think so, Peg. I can understand. I know how he felt.

Peggy: What do you mean?

Hal *shrugs.*

Spence: He was a guy who seemed to have everything. Letters in basketball and track. All-State in football. Not to mention a straight-A average.

Peggy: And he was going steady with the most popular girl in school. (*She pauses.*) It must have been horrible for his parents. They found his body, didn't they?

Spence: I heard it was the kid across the street. A seventh-grader on his way home for lunch. He looked into the Finley's yard and...

Peggy: What a terrible way to do it. A shotgun in his mouth. I don't understand it.

Hal: You don't know how that kid was pushed. The standards his parents set. It wasn't good enough that he was first string quarterback. Oh, no, he had to set all kinds of records, make the All-State team three times in a row. Man, no one can live with that.

Peggy: You're saying his parents forced him into this?

Hal: And his brothers and sister too. Look at them. His brothers both playing pro ball. His sister an Olympic swimmer. Man, he felt he couldn't match up to them.

Spence: But he did!

Hal: Not in his eyes. He had to be the best at everything he tried. You know, one time, just for fun, this pro tennis player beat him a couple of sets. Burke got so angry he smashed his racquet. Not angry at the tennis player — angry at himself. For days, he wouldn't let it go. He kept harping about how he should have won.

Peggy: That's crazy.

Hal: Maybe, but I know he couldn't help it.

Peggy: How do you know that?

Hal: We used to talk all the time.

Spence: I didn't know you two were that close.

Hal: Yeah, well, maybe we weren't. We just had a bond, a thing in common.

Peggy: What do you mean?

Hal: I've said enough. I've got to be going.

Spence: (*Trying to laugh.*) You've brought it up, you've got to tell us.

Hal: I don't know. I've been wanting to talk to someone, but...

Peggy: What is it, Hal?

Hal: I'm scared. I'm really scared.

Spence: Why, Hal? What are you scared of?

Hal: I'm afraid I'll do just what Burke did. I mean I'm depressed all the time, you know? That's what we had in common. This achievement thing. He had to be best. Well, so do I. And every time I'm not, I can't stand it. I mean, it's weird. I know nobody can be best at everything. And I don't look down on people who come in second or third or even last in anything. Except when it's me.

Peggy: I don't understand.

Hal: We had this pact, Burke and me. When either of us started feeling down, we'd call the other one right away. (*He sobs.*) Except this last time, he didn't call. You know, even though Burke set a record Friday night for most yards passing in a single game, we lost. I knew that was going to affect him. I knew somehow he'd blame himself. Just like I blame myself when things don't go right.

Spence: How did you know it would affect him that way?

Hal: (*Exasperated.*) We were so alike. When I didn't get a hundred percent on a test, when I didn't come out first in any class, the few times I lost the 100 or the 220 in track, it was like the end of the world. The end of *my* world. Burke felt that way too.

Peggy: It sounds like you blame yourself for his...for his suicide.

Hal: Yes. No. I don't know. But it's not just that. I'm scared about me, too. I don't think you can understand. I don't think anyone can understand...except someone who's been there. Someone like Burke...or like me.

Spence: I think I see. You were Burke's brake, his...control. He was the same for you. And now he's gone. Is that it?

Hal: I don't want to die. I'm so scared, and I don't want to die.

Questions for Discussion

1. Burke seemed to have everything anyone could want in life, but he killed himself. Why do you think students who "have it all" commit suicide?

2. What incident in Burke's life revealed that he probably needed to see a mental health professional?

3. In what ways does Hal compare himself to Burke?

4. If you were the peer counselor, and Hal shared his feelings with you, what steps would you take to help him?

5. Should one of Hal's friends ask him if he has a plan of action for killing himself?

Bibliography

Boskind-White, M., and W. C. White, Jr. *Bulimarexia, The Binge/Purge Cycle.* New York: W. W. Norton and Company, 1988.

Bower, Sharon, and Gordon Bower. *Asserting Yourself.* Reading, Mass.: Addison-Wesley, 1976.

Brammer, Lawrence. *The Helping Relationship: Process and Skills.* Englewood Cliffs, New Jersey: Prentice-Hall, 1973.

Bruch, H. *The Golden Cage: The Enigma of Anorexia Nervosa.* Cambridge, Mass.: Harvard University Press, 1978.

Cassady, Marsh. *Acting Step-By-Step.* San Jose, California: Resource Publications, Inc., 1988.

_____ *Characters in Action: A Guide to Play-writing.* Lanham, Maryland: University Press of America, 1984.

_____. *Playwriting Step-by-Step.* San Jose, California: Resource Publications, Inc., 1985.

D'Andrea, Vincent, and Peter Salovey. *Peer Counseling Skills and Perspectives.* Palo Alto, CA: Science and Behavior Books, 1983.

Egan, Gerald. *You and Me: The Skills of Communicating and Relating to Others.* Monterey, CA: Brooks/Cole Publishing Co., 1977.

_____. *The Skilled Helper,* 3rd ed. Monterey, CA: Brooks/Cole Publishing Co., 1977.

Furstenberg, F., Jr.; J. Menken; and R. Lincoln. *Teenage Sexuality, Pregnancy and Childbearing.* Philadelphia: University of Pennsylvania Press, 1981.

Garfinkel, P. E., and D. M. Garner. *Anorexia Nervosa: A Multidimensional Perspective.* New York: Brunner/Mazel, 1982.

Gray, H. D., and J. Tindall. *Peer Counseling: In-depth Look at Training Peer Helpers.* Muncie, Indiana: Accelerated Development, 1985.

Hebeisen, Ardyth. *Peer Program for Youth.* Minneapolis: Augsburg Publishing House, 1973.

Johnston, L. D.; J. G. Bachman; and P. O. O'Malley. *Highlights from Student Drug Use in America 1975-1981.* U.S. Department of Health and Human Services, Public Health Service, National Institute on Drug Abuse, 1982.

Kennedy, Eugene. *Crisis Counseling— The Essential Guide for Nonprofessional Counselors. New York: Continuum Publishing Company, 1986.*

Kubler-Ross, Elisabeth. *On Death and Dying.* New York: Macmillan Publishing Company, 1969.

Levenkron, S. *Treating and Overcoming Anorexia Nervosa.* New York: Warner Books, 1982.

Loughary, W. John, and Theresa M. Ripley. *Helping Others Help Themselves. New York: McGraw-Hill, 1979.*

MacFarlane, Kee, and Jill Waterman, with Shawn Conerly, Linda Damon, Michael Durfee, and Suzanne Long. *Sexual Abuse of Young Children.* New York: Guilford Publications, Inc., 1986.

Myrick, Robert D., and Tom Ervey. *Caring and Sharing.* Minneapolis: Guilford Publications, Inc., 1986.

_____. *Youth Helping Youth.* Minneapolis, Minn.: Educational Media Corp., 1980.

Myrick, Robert D., and Don L. Sorenson. *Peer Helping: A Practical Guide. Minneapolis: Educational Media Corporation, 1988.*

Peck, M. L. *Youth Suicide.* New York: Springer Publications, 1985.

Rogers, Carl. *On Becoming a Person.* Boston: Houghton-Mifflin Co., 1961.

Samuels, Mimi and Don. *The Complete Book of Peer Counseling.* Miami: Fiesta Publishing Corp., 1975.

Satir, Virginia. *Self-Esteem.* Milbrae, California: Celestial Arts, 1985.

Sturkie, Joan. *Listening with Love: True Stories from Peer Counseling.* San Jose, California: Resource Publications, Inc., 1987.

Sturkie, Joan, and Gordon R. Bear. *Christian Peer Counseling: Love in Action.* Dallas: Word, Inc., 1989.

Sturkie, Joan, and Valerie Gibson. *Peer Counselor's Handbook.* San Jose, California: Resource Publications, Inc., 1989.

Van Cleave, Stephen; Walter Byrd; and Kathy Revell. *Counseling for Substance Abuse and Addition.* Waco: Word Books, 1987.

Van Ornum, William, and John B. Mordock. *Crisis Counseling with Children and Adolescents—A Guide for Nonprofessional Counselors.* New York: Continuum Publishing Company, 1983.

Varenhorst, Barbara. *Real Friends.* San Francisco: Harper & Row, 1983.

Varenhorst, Barbara, with Lee Sparks. *Training Teenagers for Peer Ministry.* Loveland, Colorado: Group Books, 1988.

Wallerstein, J. S., and J. B. Kelly. *Surviving the Breakup: How Children and Parents Cope with Divorce.* New York: Basic Books, 1980.

Teach Teens to Listen with Love

You have just decided you want to become one of those special few who teach teens peer counseling, but you don't really know what it is all about. What is peer counseling and what happens in a peer counseling class?

Peer counseling is a unique kind of learning for teens. It encourages awareness of feelings and helps young people deal with issues like drug abuse, peer pressure, self-esteem, etc. Peer counseling also teaches teens that their peers are just as concerned about those issues as they are. But to get the real scope of what goes on in a peer counseling class, take a look at Joan Sturkie's *Listening with Love*.

Listening with Love was created by Joan Sturkie, a former high school counselor and peer counseling teacher, who now serves as a consultant for peer counseling programs. Joan shares her actual experiences as a peer counseling teacher. She gives examples of student problems and some of the problems she had to deal with herself. She illustrates through her humor and her caring that becoming a peer counseling teacher does not mean smooth sailing all the time, but she assures the reader that it is almost always rewarding.

Listening With Love can be used as part of a peer counseling class when used in conjunction with *The Teacher's Guide to Listening with Love*. For each chapter in the text, this *Teacher's Guide* presents an opening lecturette, questions for post reading, activity suggestions, and a brief preview to set readiness for the next lesson. The *Teacher's Guide* gives the peer counseling teacher a way to focus the students on their own feelings about the issues that are discussed in the stories in *Listening With Love*.

Order Form

Fill out this coupon and send it with your check or institutional purchase order to: **Resource Publications, Inc.,** 160 E. Virginia St., #290, San Jose, CA 95112. (408) 286-8505, FAX (408)287-8748.

Qty	Description	Unit Price	Amount
_____	The Peer Counselor Training Course	$49.95	_____
_____	Teacher's Guide to Listening With Love	$9.95	_____
_____	Listening With Love (paperbound)	$9.95	_____

(bulk prices from coupon on prior page apply to multiple copy purchases of Listening with Love)

California residents add 6¼% state sales tax:_____

Postage & handling ($1.75 for orders under $10, $2.25 for

orders of $10-$25, 9% (max $9) of order for orders over $25):_____

Total amount of order:_____

☐ My check or purchase order is enclosed.
☐ Charge my: ☐ Visa ☐ MC   Exp. date _____

Card #_____-_____-_____

Signature _____

Name: _____

Institution: _____

Address:_____

City: _____ St_____ Zip_____

Phone: _____

Code: AI2

Finally...You Can Help Troubled Teenagers!

THE PEER COUNSELING TRAINING COURSE

by Maggie Phillips
Edited and Revised
by Joan Sturkie

It happens all the time. You're talking to a teenager who has a long record of cutting classes and failing courses. The student simply sits in your office staring at you without any reaction to what you're saying. How can you get through to someone like that?

Answer: Through peer counseling. Peer counseling is a new way of counseling for middle school, junior high, and high school students who have problems communicating with adults.

The Peer Counseling Training Course is a teacher's guide and curriculum for middle school, junior high, and high school classes in peer counseling. Statistics show that students who take a peer counseling class have a better chance of staying in school and participating in school activities than those who do not.

Teenagers find it easier to talk about their problems with their fellow students than with adults. Through helping other teens overcome their problems, the peer counselors also gain insight about themselves.

The Peer Counseling Training Course is divided into sixteen units. Units one through nine introduce students to the skills they must learn to become good counselors. Units ten through sixteen deal with specific problems the student counselors might face, such as peer pressure, drugs, drinking, etc.

This curriculum was originally developed in the late 1970s by Maggie Phillips and formerly known as the H.O.L.D. program from the Pajaro Valley Unified School District in Watsonville, CA. Joan Sturkie, an active consultant for school peer counseling programs, has updated and edited the program to deal with AIDS and other current issues.

To order this book please use the coupon on the next page.

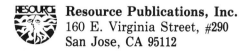

Resource Publications, Inc.
160 E. Virginia Street, #290
San Jose, CA 95112

Help for Peer Counselors

Through peer counseling, teenagers help others find their own answers to life problems.

But what happens when a peer counselor gets stuck and cannot help? What if there is no supervisor available for the peer counselor to talk to? What if the peer counselor does not remember what to do in a certain situation?

Wouldn't it be great if peer counselors could have a quick and easy guide they could refer to whenever they need help or encouragement? *The Peer Counselor's Pocket Book* is the answer.

The Peer Counselor's Pocket Book, by peer counseling consultant Joan Sturkie and peer counselor Valerie Gibson, can help any peer counselor who needs a quick and handy reference. This little book gives counseling tips, basic skills reinforcement, a referral guide, and a review of common issues peer counselors encounter.

Order Form--

To get copy(s) of *The Peer Counselor's Pocket Book* for yourself or for your class, fill out this coupon and send it along with your check or institutional purchase order to: **Resource Publications, Inc.,** 160 E. Virginia St., Suite 290, San Jose, CA 95112-5848, (408) 286-8505, FAX (408) 287-8748

Qty	Description	Unit Price	Amount
_____	*The Peer Counselor's Pocket Book* (paperbound)	_____	_____

1-25 copies $9.95 ea.   26-50 copies $8.95 ea.

51 or more $7.95 ea.

California residents add 6¼% sales tax:_____

Postage & handling ($1.75 for orders under $10, $2.25 for orders of $10-$25, 9% (max $9) of order for orders over $25):_____

Total amount of order:_____

☐ My check or purchase order is enclosed.
☐ Charge my: ☐ Visa ☐ MC   Exp. date_____

Card # _____-_____-_____-_____

Signature _____

Name: _____

Institution: _____

Street: _____

City: _____ State_____ Zip_____

Code: AI